RETAIL TRUTHS

D1316526

RETAIL TRUTHS

The UNCONVENTIONAL WISDOM *of* RETAILING

CHIP AVERWATER

ABB PRESS

Cover and type design by Erica Jennings, Jennings Design

Unattributed quotations are by Chip Averwater.

ABB Press books are available through local and online retailers. Quantity discounts are available to organizations and associations. Special editions and book excerpts can be created to specification. For more information please contact orders@abbpress.com.

For updates and more resources, visit www.retailtruths.com.

Printed in the United States of America
First Edition

ABB Press
www.abbpress.com
info@abbpress.com

Library of Congress Cataloging-in- Publication Data:
Averwater, Chip.
Retail truths: the unconventional wisdom of retailing /
Chip Averwater.

p. cm.
LCCN 2011915777
ISBN-13: 9780983979074
ISBN-10: 0983979073
1. Retail trade. I. Title.
HF5429.A94 2012   658.8'7
QBI11-600186

Dedicated to my parents,
Bob & Joan,
who have, in so many ways,
made all things possible for me.

CONTENTS

PREFACE

When I was growing up I thought everyone tended shop. It was what every adult I knew did every day. It was what I did every day I wasn't in school.

Although we called it "going to work," it never seemed like work. There were some unpleasant tasks, to be sure—loading and unloading trucks, counting inventory, housekeeping. But these were more than offset by visiting with favorite customers, showing an exciting new product, creating a beautiful display, or participating in a successful promotion. I don't remember dreading a single day.

Forty years later I'm still in love with retailing. A smoothly operating store with a steady flow of customers and healthy profits is a work of art. I still get a thrill from a big sale or a system improvement, and even enjoy poring over the numbers at month-end.

I suppose part of my infatuation is that retail has too many facets and intricacies to ever be mastered. There are thousands of lessons to learn—some critical to a store's survival, many valuable for improving customer service or increasing the store's profits, and others that simply make operations run smoother. Perhaps because I've enjoyed learning them, but also to avoid repeating my countless mistakes, I wrote many of my lessons down.

Some years ago I began gathering and polishing them. My original intention was to pass them on to my son as my father had to me and his father had to him. Perhaps it was these lessons (combined with ninety years of long hours and dogged persistence) that allowed our family musical instrument business to survive. My son would surely need them to beat the notoriously long odds facing the fourth generation.

Over the twelve years that I wrote, my co-workers unwittingly donated more lessons and examples. It seemed unfair to them (and costly to our business) not to share with them the assembled observations to which they had so generously contributed.

Then, businessmen have an irresistible urge to share their solutions—motivated, of course, more by ego than altruism. My business friends wouldn't contain their amusement if I denied my own inclinations to this. So I'll just admit that sharing with them a little collected common sense, much of which I took from them anyway, provided some of the inspiration for this effort.

Ultimately the thought crossed my mind that all of us retailers suffer the same afflictions, differing only in the widgets we peddle. Being not immune to the temptations of opportunity, I further expanded my purpose—to sell enough copies to pay for those I give away. Projects of unreasonable time and effort require delusions of unrealistic outcomes.

Failing in this lofty goal, I still have the immensely human and irresistible pleasure of dispensing advice—in this case with the added benefit of not requiring anyone to actually listen.

Please feel free to lie about enjoying it—or even having read it. I promise to enthusiastically acknowledge your compliment and not test your comprehension.

ACKNOWLEDGMENTS

As with most ideas, almost all of the thoughts collected in this book belonged to others—my mentors, associates, and friends in business. In the true tradition of business and retailing, I appropriated the ideas, forgot they weren't my own and now take credit for them.

While I can no longer match each lesson to its source, I have in no way forgotten the people and their value in shaping me.

The right place to start is with my grandfather who conceived and built the business that took me in, absorbed my errors, supplied daily practice for my lessons, and provided a living in spite of me. His gracious and patient encouragement through all my early blunders is conceivable only by his seeing some of himself in me.

My father, no doubt, paid most dearly for my business education, first in patient instruction, next in tuition and board, then in salary commensurate with the education he had himself provided, and finally in my many mistakes. As if that weren't enough, he ultimately gave me the business that was his labor of love for thirty-five years. Nothing in this world equals (or explains) parental love. His example and steady guidance was and continues to be one of my greatest treasures.

My mother, the great intellectual in my life, never met a subject she couldn't master. Indeed she often volunteered to tackle a business need we didn't know we had, as in our first computerization. In addition to the early security and curiosity that enables lifetime learning, she gave me a powerful example in study, thought, and persistence—and, most importantly, confidence to tackle any problem that vexed us.

Ron, my uncle, was my trusted friend and conscientious business partner. He showed extraordinary tolerance and restraint in allowing me to pursue projects and directions that more than occasionally proved imprudent.

My younger brother, Pat, has been a confidant and sounding board for many years. We've spent many enjoyable hours debating ideas and options and assessing our errors. Family businesses and partnerships can work just fine.

Our company has benefited immensely from some of the best managers and employees in our industry. I readily admit that they know more about their jobs than I do, and thank them for both their patience and the many lessons they've taught me.

Several business sharing groups (MIIG, KEG, Big Eight, NAMM, NASMD) taught me and confirmed by example many of the lessons I've recorded here. Being privy to the intricate details, financials, and personalities of other similar businesses is as close to the experience of running multiple businesses as one can get while running just one. My friends in these groups have been wellsprings of ideas, fertile testing grounds, powerful illustrations of what (and sometimes what not) to do, often inspiration, more often commiserators, the best of drinking buddies, and the most experienced and knowledgeable board of directors in our industry.

My wife, Jan, provided far more encouragement, support

and understanding than I deserved. Too many nights she waited patiently while I finished one more paragraph before supper or bed. There could never be a more compatible or compassionate soulmate.

And finally, my children provided the inspiration for saving these thoughts. Much of my life has been lived through them; I've enjoyed every minute and the outcome is my greatest source of pride.

"The secret to creativity is knowing how to hide your sources."

—Albert Einstein

RETAIL IS DETAIL

I was standing at the front of our musical instrument store not long ago when a boy rode up on his bike and came in. The salespeople were busy so I asked him how I could help. He asked me several questions and then said, "You mus' be da owner here." I smiled and said, "You're a pretty smart little guy. How'd you know that?" He said, "Cuz you don't know nothin'."

It was an astute observation. I often feel that way, especially on the sales floor.

Yet I believe there are many things every surviving retailer learns.

Some are the complex concepts taught in business schools—double-entry accounting, contract law, creating financial statements, etc.

But far more are the practical insights and techniques gathered only on the frontline—negotiating with suppliers, choosing among job applicants, setting profitable prices, resolving employee disputes, sending messages to competitors, designing motivational incentive plans, firing employees, attracting bankers …. We learn these one-at-a-time, in the trenches, under-fire, and with considerable costs and consequences.

Many of my lessons were drilled into me by my father and grandfather, who hoped, for their sake and mine, I wouldn't need to repeat them. Others were shared or offered by example by my retailer friends (and a few enemies); vicariously is cost-effective learning if we just pay attention. Most, unfortunately, I paid full price for; lessons, it seems, are more convincing and memorable when we fully appreciate their consequences.

And now I pass my lessons on to you. You will, of course, have to test each one for yourself—truths ring true only with experience. But perhaps you'll recognize them more readily and more affordably than I did.

> "We are generally better persuaded by the reasons we discover ourselves than by those given to us by others."
>
> —Blaise Pascal

It looks so easy
to be so hard.

Rent a space, order some merchandise, run an ad, and operate the cash register. Anybody can do that!

Apparently not. Estimates of the retailing failure rate range as high as 95 percent. And for those who fail, not only are their hard work and long hours unrewarded but, in most cases, their precious bets—usually their life savings—are lost.

Easy work and guaranteed returns are not in the description of retail.

It's not whether we can do it; it's whether we can do it best.

The challenge isn't in merely offering products the public wants to buy; we've got to do it better than all of our competitors.

Each shopper chooses only one store for his purchase, the one he feels offers the best value—not just quality and price but convenience, selection, security, atmosphere, etc.

The winner takes all. Second place gets nothing, no matter how great the effort or how close the race.

Retailing isn't one skill.

Try to define the skills of a successful retailer. We can create a list but regardless of its length it's inevitably incomplete.

A retailer needs abilities in sales, marketing, management, accounting, advertising, purchasing, hiring, training, finance, negotiating, collection, dispute resolution, public relations, real estate, insurance, law, and much more.

Specialists such as accountants and lawyers can provide some valuable expertise. But it's still the retailer who has to determine what advice to seek, how much he can afford, whose advice to accept, how much of it to apply, and how to balance it with other aspects of the business with which it inevitably conflicts.

> We've gotten so much good advice through the years it's a wonder we're still in business.

So few ways to succeed and so many ways to fail.

Ultimately there is only one way we can succeed in retail: provide products our customers want better than all of our competitors.

But there are countless ways we can get into trouble—uncontrolled expenses, buying mistakes, theft and fraud, unmotivated personnel, inadequate collection, poor people-management, pricing too high, pricing too low, bad product selection, ignorance of laws, too many or too few employees, inaccurate financial projections, overly optimistic expansions …. All the world conspires against a retailer.

With profits typically 1-3 percent of sales, the margin for error is frighteningly small. Every mistake is serious; combinations can be fatal.

The battles are decided on details.

Competition assures that differences between stores are small. Products are similar, sometimes identical; pricing is necessarily close; policies, methods, and hours are often indistinguishable.

Yet the shopper must choose. It's her money and she's determined to get the best value for it.

But on what criteria? With so much the same, little is left but details: location, décor, displays, signage, organization, cleanliness, knowledge and politeness of salespeople, speed of check-out, ease of return, width of aisles, background music, and a thousand other mundane—but critical—details.

The plan is simple; execution is the challenge.

Knowing how a store should operate isn't hard. Our customers can tell us that (and often do when things aren't going smoothly). The art of retailing is getting everything right at the same time and within budget.

It's more acrobatics than rocket science. But the acrobats are spinning too many plates to ever be perfect.

He who spins his plates most consistently wins the sale.

One of my favorite Chinese suppliers often says: "Talk doesn't cook rice." Nor does a retail plan operate a store.

A good retailer is a compulsive improver.

Discontent is the driving force of retail. A retailer tweaks and fine-tunes his business, determined to make every feasible enhancement he can conceive or plagiarize.

Nothing exists in retail that can't be improved: displays can be more attractive and descriptive; salespeople can know more about the products and about human relations; marketing can deliver a more stimulating message to a more promising audience; products can be more attractive and less expensive; selections can be broadened; stock-outs can be reduced; paperwork can be more efficient; handling can be reduced; shrinkage can be decreased; collections can be sped up; bad debts can be reduced; customer relationships can be broadened and deepened ....

A retailer is often tired but never bored.

Impatience is a virtue.

Once conceived, an improvement can't be made soon enough; if it's a good idea, we should have already done it. Delays are simply intolerable.

We no sooner finish one project than we undertake the next, all with a sense of emergency. (This do-it-now urgency is a great source of frustration to those we charge with implementing our seemingly endless stream of brainchildren.)

There's pride in each accomplishment, but there's just no time to dwell on it—we've discovered other imperfections and opportunities and so much remains to be done.

> A psychologist once told me that motivation is a burden since a motivated person is never satisfied.
>
> On the other hand, "Success is a journey," and every step forward is a joy.

There's no finish line.

No retailer gets all the details right. Those who claim to are either "puffing" in their advertising or sales, or fantasizing, and need a strong dose of their customers' perceptions to shock them back to reality.

Even if it were possible, the feat would be short-lived; our competitors would quickly copy our formulas and techniques, close the gap, and require us to add new details and methods to again separate us from the pack.

Retailing is constantly evolving and improving. The best stores of ten years ago are out-of-date in today's markets.

There is no ultimate store, no ultimate service, no ultimate customer experience—and no rest for the retailer.

10

The details we miss would have been our profit.

Expenses typically absorb 97-99 percent of retail revenue. The 1-3 percent that remains as profit is tiny by comparison (but infinitely more desirable than the sea of red numbers that are possible).

We don't have to get all the details right, but each one we miss comes directly off the bottom line. And it doesn't take many missed details to turn the numbers red.

> "Here you have to run as fast as you can to stay where you are. If you want to get some place else, you have to run much faster."
>
> —**Red Queen,** *Alice in Wonderland*

11

A store is a portrait of its owner.

Perhaps most people wouldn't consider a retail store a work of art. But a store is indeed an artistic creation, emanating from the founder's vision, interpreted and shaped according to his talents and skills, and made inevitably unique in its innumerable details.

The individual character of a store develops and evolves gradually—the accumulation of many large and small decisions we make (or ignore) over the course of its existence.

We rarely step back during the process to recognize the creation accruing from our daily efforts. But eventually every characteristic of the store—location, décor, staff, products, displays, organization, policies, methods, marketing, etc.—has been determined, directly or indirectly, by its owner.

The owner's vision is adopted by the staff, his priorities become the goals, his habits become the standards, and his style becomes the culture. Despite his (politically savvy) protests that many people play roles, he is indeed the producer and the product is his.

If you want to know the owner, walk through his store.

12

You must be present to win.

To be successful a retailer doesn't have to be brilliant, highly educated, charismatic, refined, or unusually talented. But he must mind the store.

Luck, ideas, relationships and even intelligence are dwarfs in retail next to effort. The winner is almost always the most focused and dedicated. Success is the product of hard work and long hours.

Retailers who are irresistibly distracted by hobbies, personal and family problems, civic and industry associations, charities, and outside business ventures pay dearly for their diversions. A well-established store can sometimes survive a little inattention but when ignored long enough its momentum turns in the wrong direction; less-rooted stores seldom survive anything less than full focus for even short periods.

A successful retailer can usually be found in his store. An 8-hour day isn't long enough; taking off is out of the question.

13

It's not work when it's fun.

A good retailer is passionate about his business. He thrives on constant improvement, delights in innovation, savors the challenges, and relishes the competition.

The store is his child and his creation, the embodiment of his ideas and beliefs. He celebrates its sales, its improvements, and its competitive victories, and agonizes over every inefficiency, lost sale, and disappointed customer.

Not every day is a win, but the losses make the wins sweeter. He sometimes goes to bed defeated but he wakes up renewed and resolved to take up the fight again.

> "When you like your work, every day is a holiday."
>
> —Frank Tyger

SELLING

14

Salesmanship is 90 percent preparation, 10 percent presentation.

Good salesmanship begins before the customer arrives. Salespeople need knowledge, training, and rehearsal—before helping customers.

Unfortunately, retail seldom allows time and expense for that ideal. Too often our salespeople get their training on the sales floor, searching for information and answers beside our customers, and learning their communication skills from their mistakes.

Tricks and gimmicks don't sell; knowledge and communication do.

The fast-talking, back-slapping salesman stereotype might have been accurate at one time, but it isn't appropriate today. Tricking and cajoling customers into buying products they don't need just doesn't work. Customers are too smart to be tricked, refund policies ensure those sales don't stay sold, and such a store's reputation and trade would quickly deteriorate.

The art of retail selling is straightforward:

- Create rapport with the customer
- Collect information to define his need
- Match the need to appropriate products
- Communicate the options and differences
- Maintain focus on the decision
- Facilitate the financial transaction
- Ensure satisfaction

It really isn't any more complicated than that—but that doesn't mean it's easy.

Expecting to get the sale is half of getting it.

Confidence is contagious; unfortunately, so is lack of confidence.

A relaxed and assured manner fosters trust and communication. Customers subconsciously sense a salesperson's attitude and assume it's based on his confidence in his products and recommendations.

Conversations tend to mesh in style, attitude, and focus. When a customer perceives a salesperson's expectation that the conversation will culminate in a sale, he tends to adopt that expectation himself.

Confidence goes a long way in explaining how a salesperson can "get on a roll" and why busy salespeople typically have higher closing ratios.

> Whatever the product or environment, knowledge and confidence have always led the way in sales. A salesman who lacks either is just a clerk.

Confidence must be earned.

Some self-confidence is innate in personalities. Most is earned through study and practice.

The first step for a salesperson is learning the products. He has to be familiar enough with features and benefits to make quick summary comparisons and accurately match products with customer needs.

Then he has to practice his presentation of this information (preferably not on customers) until it becomes second nature.

A salesperson who knows and believes in the product and can present the information comfortably is naturally confident.

> Every time we send a salesman for concentrated product training, his sales of the product jump to a new level.
>
> The products haven't changed—only his understanding and confidence have. And they are highly persuasive to a customer with a product need.

18

Knowledge speaks, wisdom listens.

Great salespeople are easy to spot; they listen when their customers speak. They know that what the customer says is more important than what they say. And when they listen they learn what the customer needs and will buy.

Listening builds trust and lowers customers' apprehension, defensiveness, and resistance. Customers' reluctance to talk to salespeople is due largely to salespeople's reputation (sometimes deserved) for being more interested in selling what they have than what the customer needs or wants. Asking and listening attentively is the obvious solution.

But listening requires discipline and self-restraint. When a strong sales point comes to mind, we're naturally eager to present it. A good salesperson resists that urge until the timing is right. When a customer speaks, he stops what he's saying—often mid-sentence—no matter how important his thought. He knows a customer who is talking isn't listening. If the idea is important, it will get better consideration if he holds it for a more receptive moment.

The best communication is a relationship.

Customers buy from salespeople they know and like. They listen to them, they trust them, and they want to do business with them.

Good salespeople are aware of this and work hard to build personal relationships. They get customers' names and use them often. They make their own name easy for customers to remember by repeating it, offering a similarity ("Chip, like a potato chip or a computer chip"), inserting it in conversation, wearing a name tag, giving business cards, writing it on sales literature, etc.

They look for commonalities and connections—people, occupations, schools, hobbies, backgrounds, children. They keep a file of customer information and study it often so they recognize and remember their customers when they return and can easily make conversation.

And after a sale they follow up to ensure their customer is happy. A buyer doesn't become a previous customer but a friend, key influencer, and future customer.

> Among the best salespeople I've worked with through the years, a common denominator has been a dependable memory (or system) for names and faces, a warm and welcoming manner, and an eagerness to listen and help.

There is no magic close.

Retail salespeople sometimes talk about "closing" as though what the salesperson says at the end of the conversation makes everything that came before it irrelevant. "He's getting customers; he just doesn't know how to close them."

There is no secret combination of words or mystic phrase that causes customers to buy indiscriminately. A customer buys when all the pieces are in place: he has a need, the need is correctly identified, suitable products are shown, he believes a product matches his need, he feels the price is fair, the money is available ....

True, once an appropriate product is identified, the salesperson should maintain focus on a decision and ask what else needs to be done to facilitate the sale. Many customers need that encouragement.

However, if any of the requisite steps haven't been adequately completed, there is no (legal) phrase that will make the customer buy. The problem is not in the "close" but in the steps that came before it.

A return policy is a tool, not a rule.

The purpose of a return policy is to encourage sales, not to limit when and how customers can return something they're unhappy with. "Take it with you. If you don't like it, you can bring it back."

Smart retailers don't reluctantly offer return policies—they promote and advertise them. Not only do such policies create more sales, but if a customer is unhappy with a purchase, we don't want him to keep it and be continually reminded of the bad experience with our store.

We have to forget about the few who abuse a return policy and focus on those who buy more because of the reassurance. The cost of a return is negligible if the merchandise isn't damaged. And even those who buy intending to return often don't get around to it or change their minds and keep the product.

> In the '80s a chain of electronics stores, McDuff's, had its salespeople greet customers at the door with a printed copy of their liberal return policy and low price guarantee. Presumably they recognized that those two policies eliminated most hesitancy to purchase.

Be-backs don't come back.

A rookie counts "be backs" as future sales; veterans recognize them as missed sales.

"I'll be back" is what customers say to extricate themselves from the situation without disappointing the salesperson. Even those customers who believe they'll come back seldom do; they get distracted, lose their motivation, find other options, or simply procrastinate.

When a customer says he'll be back or asks for a card, we should ask if we've shown him the correct product, answered his questions, and provided enough information. If he answers yes, he'll typically say he just needs to think about it, which translates as "I'm not yet convinced that this is the right product or best price." If he is receptive to further discussion, we should continue asking questions and providing information.

If the customer declines to continue the conversation, we can offer to send him some literature, collect some additional information for him, or call him if it goes on sale.

Follow-up is the great divide between average and outstanding salesmen.

Following up means staying in touch with prospective buyers, calling, mailing, or emailing with additional information, keeping the purchase active in the customer's mind, and providing whatever help the customer needs to make his decision.

For big ticket merchandise, it's virtually impossible to be a top salesperson without consistent follow-up. It can as much as double or triple sales.

A salesperson should always have a helpful reason for calling or mailing—collected more information about the product, availability, options, or pricing; located an alternative product they might be interested in; an invitation to a coming event; an upcoming sale …. Reasons are abundant when the salesman has determination.

Our piano department stages a variety of follow-up contests. In one they set a goal of six follow-up calls per day per salesperson. Each person who doesn't make his six calls in a day puts a dollar in the pot. The company puts in $10 for the week. At the end of the week the salesperson with the most follow-ups gets 60 percent of the pot, the second most 40 percent. The amount of money isn't the attraction; it's the pride (or dishonor) of the outcome.

Not surprisingly, the winner each week almost always has the highest sales too.

"Satisfied" is a slow way to build business.

Surveys of retail customers often list "satisfied" as the highest possible rating of a retail experience. It's no wonder unhappy customers tell more people about their experiences than happy customers.

Customers are at best "satisfied" because companies almost never do more than they promise.

We don't need satisfied customers; we need customers who are surprised and impressed.

Salespeople have lots of opportunities to exceed a customer's expectations: help him with his initial use of the product, send a thank you note, add a bow and a card to a delivery, estimate 2-week order delivery and deliver in 10 days, refer someone to the customer in his business ....

I once hired a landscaper to build a wall and terrace. When he finished he proudly showed me some steps he had added that weren't part of our agreement. He told me he liked to give his customers more than he promised so they'd remember him.

It's been more than twenty years but I still remember his name and have recommended him to many people. I suspect he's recovered the costs of those steps many times over.

Just because they don't complain doesn't mean they're happy.

Customers don't like to be complainers. Some would rather stew in their dissatisfaction, tell their friends and neighbors about it and swear off any further business with us than tell us they're unhappy.

A retailer can't afford many unhappy customers. His market is his community. He depends on relationships and his reputation in the community for continuing business.

Many smart retailers take no chances; they contact their customers and ask if they're happy.

Complaints are opportunities to create loyal customers.

Ever notice that our most loyal customers are often those who once had a complaint that we resolved? (Should we screw up more often just so we can fix it?)

A little attention usually makes up for a mistake, and our concern and determination to make it right demonstrate our standards and trustworthiness. The resulting relationship is a bond competitors can't easily break.

A local violin teacher gave us fits for a while. She laid out precise specifications for the instruments we rented to her students and expected each instrument to come with some unusual accessories and music.

We were happy to accommodate, of course. But if any of our salespeople in any of our stores didn't catch that a renter was her student or overlooked any detail, I was sure to get a scorching phone call and extensive scolding.

To make things more challenging, this teacher refused to set foot in our stores or have a civil phone conversation. She wanted nothing to do with us and seemed hell-bent on proving our stupidity to everyone.

After a couple of months of this, I bought a country ham and a Christmas card and knocked on her door. I had to introduce myself as we'd never met. She was completely off-guard and asked several times why I was bringing her a ham. I said it was to thank her for her patience—a poor choice of words since she obviously had none, but she accepted the ham just the same.

From that day forward she was one of our most loyal music teachers, sending innumerable customers to us with specific lists of merchandise to rent or buy (most of which far exceeded the cost of a ham). When she retired we felt it all the way to the bottom line.

A satisfaction guarantee is an insurance policy on your reputation.

Making sure our customers are happy isn't just good ethics, it's good economics. A dissatisfied customer is costly as he'll likely influence many other potential customers.

Unhappy customers often imagine the store will resist a remedy or refund. Anticipation of a battle sometimes builds enough that the salesperson can sense the animosity when the customer finally reports the problem.

Other customers who fear an unpleasant confrontation never bring the problem to our attention. Instead they resign themselves to the faulty product and are reminded of their "mistake" every time they see or use it.

Satisfaction guarantees help us head off hard feelings and encourage unhappy customers to allow us to resolve the problem.

Some years ago we proposed a generous satisfaction policy—so generous that it raised the concerns of our managers and salespeople. They felt some customers would take advantage of it by buying new instruments to use for weekend gigs and returning them used. As a result we couldn't develop a consensus to adopt it.

Finally, without any announcement, we adjusted the software to print the new policy on the bottom of every receipt. It took the staff a couple of weeks to notice it; when they did, we told them we were just trying it.

We've been trying it for years. It's become part of most sales presentations and I suspect the salespeople would resist any suggestion to give it up.

28

Pricing is the delicate balance between making sales and making a profit.

Every retailer is torn between selling for less to create sales and selling for more to create profits. Survival depends on finding the narrow ground between.

But that thin space isn't clearly defined. The price at which profits disappear isn't just the wholesale cost—it must include a share of the many individual expenses incurred by the business.

Even when we know where our prices should stop, our competitors often don't. Sometimes they're too inexperienced to recognize it; sometimes they miscalculate it; most often they simply don't do the math. They eventually succumb to their lack of profitability, but it matters little since they're soon replaced by another with all the same lessons to learn.

Ultimately only those retailers survive who correctly estimate the balance point and have the discipline to maintain it despite competitors' miscalculations.

Pricing is science in theory, art in practice.

Every businessperson and economics student is familiar with the price/demand curve—as prices go down sales go up; as prices go up sales go down. Theoretically it's possible, given a perfectly controlled retail environment and time to experiment, to determine the point on the curve at which price and sales create maximum profit.

But ideal conditions and time to experiment come true only in textbooks. In the real world we take our best guesses: "I think customers will be willing to pay this much for this product." "Considering all of our costs, I don't think we can sell it for less than this."

We assume that our guesses were pretty close when we make a net profit, but we can never know how close. Only experience and feel for the market keep us within a profitable range.

The right price isn't a multiple of wholesale.

Some retailers have a sense for pricing that both enhances their profits and creates customers. Others price according to an old and unsophisticated rule of thumb—fixed percentage markup from wholesale.

Percentage markup assumes that all of the expenses of a sale are determined by the product's wholesale cost. While a few are (cost of capital, insurance, etc.), far more are functions of labor, occupancy, support, and all the other expenses of retail.

Pricing correctly means individually and by feel, with consideration given to the total expenses of the sale, customers' price sensitivity, competitive options, and the sale's potential contribution to other business.

Only occasionally and by coincidence should markup percentages match.

Larry Thomas, former co-president of the Guitar Center chain, offered his trainees an anecdote: You find a $10 bill on the street. It cost you nothing. If someone offers you $5 for it, should you take it? Why not?

The last few percentage points are the profit.

According to the US Economic Census, the net profit of a retailer after everyone and everything else are paid is typically 1-3 percent of total sales.

When we're too aggressive in our pricing, give unnecessary discounts, or make any of the myriad mistakes in buying and selling, a sale easily turns into a loss—and the loss isn't limited to the 1-3 percent we hoped to make. We dig deeply into our back pockets to pay for each of out mistakes.

A rookie retailer doesn't sense the price of his mistakes as he makes them—they're obscured in an ocean of transactions. But after a few year-ends in which he contemplates miniscule or negative returns for his year of labor, his mistakes take on painful new meaning.

Volume feeds egos, profit feeds families.

Chasing sales becomes so habitual and impulsive for retailers that we sometimes forget that the goal is not making more sales but making a profit. The two don't necessarily go together—when we price too low they're inversely related.

Many business fables tell of retailers being "busy until the day we went out of business." No matter how many times we've heard the lesson, the irony of losing money while making sales continues to surprise and amuse us.

A wise retailer doesn't set goals only for the top line of the financial statement; he focuses equal attention on the critical lines below. Only the combination determines whether and how his efforts are rewarded.

Wholesale is the cost of the merchandise, not the cost of the sale.

The price paid the manufacturer is only the first of many expenses in a transaction. Sales can't be made without expenses for rent, salaries, advertising, utilities, telephones, freight, maintenance, taxes ....

Just because a sale has a gross margin doesn't mean it's profitable. Unless the price covers all of the sale's expenses we take money out of our pockets to make it.

Which sales should bear the operating expenses?

Many salesmen and some managers subscribe to the notion of incremental sales and profits: "Our expenses are fixed so we should accept every sale that has a positive gross margin."

It would be nice to fix expenses; unfortunately increases in sales require increases in personnel, space, inventory, handling, and virtually every other expense of doing business. The increases aren't always in a smooth progression, but they're depressingly reliable. (If our expenses don't increase on one extra sale, on which sale do they?)

In highly competitive retail fields like new-car sales, savvy shoppers are often able to negotiate deals that avoid their share of costs, and dealers make it up on unwary buyers. The public recognizes the innate unfairness of this and the dealer's (and the industry's) reputation suffers.

Every sale incurs operating expenses and its price should be sufficient to cover them plus a fair contribution to profit.

A good retailer is an avid mathematician.

A retailer needs a clear idea of his costs in every sale, service, and activity his store engages in. The information is critical not only in setting prices but in deciding what to stock, what to promote, and where to channel the store's investment and efforts.

A "feel" for costs is never accurate; a business has too many expenses to remember and we chronically underestimate them. (Otherwise we wouldn't complain so unpleasantly when the bills come in.)

For a true understanding of costs, we have to periodically sit down with a spreadsheet and divide the whole list of expenses across our sales of products and services. Only then do our costs become clear.

There is always someone to ensure we're not the low price.

Weaker competitors instinctively know they'll be the customers' choice only if they offer lower prices. Many simply set their prices below the other stores as a matter of habit. Instead of understanding their costs they grasp at every potential sale and cross their fingers that there will be a little profit left when the dust settles.

It's futile and suicidal to try to price below these competitors—when you drop your price, they drop theirs further.

Most of us have been tempted to help them destroy their pesky businesses by pushing prices lower. It's a pleasant daydream but a costly and usually ineffective tactic. New competitors would quickly fill the void like the never-ending swarm of mosquitoes from a forest. And prices often become entrenched at the lower levels and are difficult to restore to reasonableness.

Differentiation is almost always a better strategy— offer better products and services that customers are willing to pay more for.

It's sometimes possible (and often satisfying) to confuse your competitors and frustrate their efforts to underprice you.

One of our managers routinely printed higher price-lists before the beginning of each back-to-school season and sent copies to our competitors' favorite customers and allies.

He released his real pricelist only on the first day of the season. Competitors who caught it then could either scramble to reset their prices and revise their advertising or stay with their higher pricing.

He who underestimates his costs gets the sale.

When multiple retailers are pitted against one another in price wars and bidding, there's almost always one who misjudges his expenses and "wins" the sale at an unprofitable price.

A little thought and calculation might allow him to discover his errors. Most, however, never separate their low-margin sales and expenses from the rest, and repeat their mistakes as long as their other sales can support their errors.

Many seasoned retailers don't bother to bid against naïve competitors—they feel their time is better spent elsewhere.

Sensible pricing is the responsibility of the market leader.

Unless the players in a market are strongly differentiated, only the leader can afford to initiate new pricing. Stores without positive differentiation must fall in line below him.

As a result the market leader has a critical responsibility to understand his costs and adjust his prices as necessary. Obsession with the pricing of those behind him only sets off a death spiral.

Low margin sales take potentially profitable sales off the market. They set precedents with our customers, our salespeople, and our competitors. When we refuse them, we sometimes get the deals at more logical prices.

Reputations are made on price sensitive items, margins on the rest.

Price sensitive items are those bought frequently and advertised often. In a grocery store they might be bread, milk, and soft drinks; in a musical instrument store they include strings, reeds, and picks. Because customers buy them often, price differences are more apparent.

Pricing these items low creates a value image for the store. Higher margins on other merchandise allow the store to cover its expenses, stay in business, and occasionally even make a profit.

(If you have trouble reconciling this idea with the idea that each sale should cover its own expenses, think of price-sensitive items as an advertising and promotion expense.)

It won't sell if it's not on sale.

Customers have become so accustomed to sales that many won't make a significant purchase unless the product is on sale.

Some furniture and clothing stores schedule only brief intervals between sales which they use to catch up, restock, organize, and collect prospects for the next sale. Many department stores end one sale only as the next begins.

(Consumer protection laws prohibit posting a "regular price" next to the sale price unless you can show that you actually sell the product at the regular price on occasion.)

But if merchandise is always "on sale," is a sale really a sale? Shoppers apparently don't ponder the question too long; most are grateful to have purchase rationalization so conveniently provided.

Holding onto inventory mistakes only makes them more costly.

Buying mistakes, technology and fashion evolution, and other demand changes cause dead inventory to accumulate and threaten to bury us.

Typically we recognize the problem but resist the solution. We hold onto our mistakes, irrationally hoping customers will appear looking for just such outdated, overpriced merchandise and bail us out of our problems. Occasionally it happens, but seldom is it worth the holding costs (investment, space, insurance, shrinkage, missed opportunity, etc.).

A product's value is determined by the market. What we paid for the product is not a factor in what it will sell for and should not influence our willingness to sell it for what it's worth now. It's almost always more profitable to move it out and put the investment and floor space to more productive use.

Our cost is a criterion in whether we stock the item again and what we would pay for it, but not in what we can sell this item for. The mistake was in buying; trying to make up for it in selling only makes the mistake more costly.

Margins are neither guaranteed nor restricted.

For whatever reason we tend to think our prices should fall within a sacred range of markup. Pricing above that range stirs guilt; having to take a reduction from it makes us feel cheated.

Consider that the value of a house is what it will sell for in the market. The price the owner paid for it some years ago isn't relevant. Buyers compare and choose from the houses available; if a house is priced competitively, it sells; if it's priced too high, it remains on the market. How the seller comes out is not a consideration in the buyer's decision.

When a product suddenly becomes obsolete, the manufacturer lowers its suggested price, or a competitor slashes its market price, our inventory cost is not our customers' concern. If we want to sell the product, we have to price it to the current market.

Similarly, when we make a special purchase, find an advantageous source, import directly, or buy in large quantities, our selling price shouldn't be determined by our cost. We can, if we like, pass the savings on to our customers in hopes of making additional sales. Or we can ask the market price—and make up for some of those sales in which we took a loss or short margin.

PROFIT

Profit is not immoral.

Some people feel that selling something for more than was paid for it is somehow dishonest—that a company can be profitable only by ripping off its customers.

They view every transaction as a zero-sum game: one party wins only when the other loses. They don't recognize that in a good transaction both parties benefit— both get something they would rather have than what they gave to get it.

A shopper chooses the best value available to him to meet his particular need. The store that anticipated the need and met it more attractively than its competitors gets the sale. The store's profit isn't due to ripping the customer off; it's the store's payment (and incentive) for anticipating and meeting the customer's need.

If the customer is unhappy with his purchase, he'll stop buying from the store. If the store is unhappy with its profit, it will stop selling the product or serving the market. But if both are satisfied, they'll continue doing business together.

Profit is far from immoral. It's the most effective and efficient economic incentive yet devised and has created for all of us the highest standards of living the world has ever known.

> "Some regard private enterprise as if it were a predatory tiger to be shot. Others look upon it as a cow that they can milk. Only a handful see it for what it really is— the strong horse that pulls the whole cart."
>
> **—Winston Churchill**

A retailer deserves payment for his work, too.

No one expects a painter to paint his house for the cost of the paint, a yardman to mow his lawn for the cost of the gasoline, or a carpenter to build his house for the cost of the lumber. Nor should anyone expect a retailer to tend a store for the cost of the merchandise.

Retailers and their salespeople have families to support and bills to pay too. Profit on their sales is their income—the only source of revenue to pay for the services they provide.

Profit is to a retailer what a wage is to a workman, a tip to a waiter, and a salary to a school teacher.

Our profit isn't a criterion in our customer's decision.

When a customer needs a product, he compares the offerings in the market and selects the best value for his money. If he perceives our offer to be the best available to him, he buys from us. What we paid for the merchandise isn't a factor in his choice.

Sales are an indication a retailer is providing a valuable service—a better value than otherwise available in the market. If he's able to make a profit in the process, he's earned it. It allows and encourages him to provide the service.

Knowledgeable people understand the necessity and fairness of profits. Those who don't should be a source of embarrassment to themselves, not to us.

> "Profit...(is) a vote of confidence from society that what is offered by the firm is valued."
>
> **—Konosuke Matsushita**

Profit is the fraction that sometimes remains after everyone else is paid.

A retailer's largest expense is to his manufacturers for the merchandise he sells—typically 55-75 percent of sales income, according to the 2007 US Economic Census. He pays his employees 12-20 percent of sales, plus benefits of 2-4 percent of sales. Then there's rent, utilities, and insurance, amounting to 3-8% of sales. Telephones, advertising, office supplies, computers and equipment, accounting, and a hundred other miscellaneous expenses typically take 8-14 percent. And then there are the unexpected expenses, the only surprise being which ones and how much.

Will there be anything left? That's the question that deprives a retailer of significant sleep. It creates his notorious obsession with expenses and earns him his reputation as "frugal," "scrooge," "tight bastard," and some less printable.

If sales are good and a retailer manages expenses carefully, he might achieve the 1-3 percent net profit the Economic Census says is average (before the government takes as much as half).

When things don't go as well, he works for free or takes a loss. And, as many unsuccessful retailers can attest, while competition and taxes restrict profits, the losses have no limits.

Profit is not a luxury.

A business that doesn't make a profit isn't a business long.

Profit allows us to continue our work. It lets us take care of our customers as both we and they think they should be. It allows us to pay competitive wages and offer health and retirement benefits. Profit lets us maintain and improve the workplace.

Ironically those who feel a business shouldn't earn a profit are the ones who feel most cheated when an unprofitable company cuts wages and benefits or goes out of business, leaving employees without work.

> "It is a socialist idea that making a profit is a vice; I consider the real vice is making losses."
>
> **—Winston Churchill**

Profit is the sum of a thousand little improvements.

On rare occasions a product is so desirable and competition so limited that a store can turn a profit regardless of how well it executes. Some of us stand in long lines to get the latest electronics, newest video game, or hot Christmas toy because it's the only way to get something we want badly. But those situations are rare and short-lived.

In the normal retail world having the product is only the starting line of the competition and gets us nowhere close to break-even. Turning the bottom line from red to black requires a combination of many little details— effective advertising, convenient location, attractive displays, knowledgeable salespeople, visible signage, reliable systems, quick checkout ....

The formula isn't secret. It just requires continuous attention, hard work, and persistence.

Profits are for growth,
not vacations and extravagance.

A store needs profit not so the owners or investors can buy yachts and winter in the Caribbean but to grow inventories, expand locations, add personnel, upgrade systems, improve facilities ....

A successful business grows, with or without management's consent. Products and services that appeal to existing customers attract more customers. Stopping a retail store from growing or contracting is as difficult as holding a boat still in a current—you're always moving, forward or backward. In retailing, backward is dangerous; forward is preferable but expensive—it requires profits.

Profit makes a better workplace.

Profit allows a store to pay higher wages, provide better benefits and perks, afford new technologies, and create a more comfortable and attractive work environment.

Profit relieves constant performance pressures and avoids looming threats of layoffs and dismissals; it gives management and employees latitude to try innovative ideas and promotions and to expand into new opportunities and products. It affords the personnel and equipment needed to serve customers well and create a base of customers who respect and appreciate the store and its employees.

Creating a good workplace is much easier when we have profits to work with.

Profit is every employee's business.

Managers who assume employees aren't interested in or can't handle profit information underestimate their people. It would be a poor employee who never gave a thought to the store's need to sell for more than what it pays.

Without access to actual numbers employees envision the store's gross margin to be mostly net profit, and they assume the owner takes it home—profoundly wrong data for decision making as well as for engendering commitment.

With the exception of individual payroll information (which everyone expects to be confidential but rarely is), a P&L contains few numbers that are critically sensitive. Employees can not only understand income and expense items but can directly influence many of them.

CUSTOMER PERSPECTIVES

Retail doesn't get rave reviews.

Most shoppers agree that the typical retail experience isn't good. Many say they hate to shop—stores are crowded, parking is distant, help is rarely available, lines are long, salespeople don't know the products ....

It's strange and unfortunate that retail can't rate better satisfaction, especially considering the army of talented business people focused on it. Maybe it's that consumers experience retailing almost daily and become highly discriminating in their standards. Or perhaps they see excellent examples of particular aspects of retailing individually, but rarely does any retailer get it all right at once.

More likely it's that a store with ideal facilities and an abundance of top quality salespeople is too expensive to be competitive.

Whatever the reason, a retailer can expect little sympathy from his customers. Their patience is thin, their budgets stretched, and they are ever-conscious of their power to take their business elsewhere.

They crave the low price but curse the poor service.

Most shoppers subconsciously recognize the realities of price/service trade-offs—they can have low prices or they can have good service, but not both.

Great service in retailing isn't a secret formula—it's mostly a matter of quantity and quality of employees. A retailer who wants to improve service simply hires more and better people. And all would, if price competition didn't constrain expenses. The challenge is in finding the balance between service and price that appeals to customers.

When customers choose a store they're choosing the service and amenities they're willing to pay for. But just having to choose is frustrating. Everyone wants to believe they can get low prices without compromises in service. Occasionally it works out; often it leads to disappointment and dissatisfaction.

Expectations rise with every contact.

The last experience is the new standard.

Attentive salespeople make an impression today, but if they're not available tomorrow it's not only a missed opportunity—the customer feels slighted. New displays and fresh décor impress a customer on the first visit or two but soon are hardly noticed; when décor deteriorates, the store is perceived in decline. A consistent record of having what the customer needs only makes a stock-out more disappointing.

In retail, maintaining service, systems and facilities isn't enough. Only continuous improvement keeps customers.

No retailer ever won a battle with a customer.

OK, it's true—customers are sometimes just wrong. They misunderstand products, what a store can do, how business is done, or what pricing is realistic. Sometimes they seem totally unreasonable.

But even when our logic is flawless and our facts undeniable, presenting them doesn't get the results we want. If we show customers they're wrong or how much they don't know, we only embarrass them and increase their unhappiness with us.

It's almost always more productive to swallow our pride, apologize for the perceived injustice, and make it "right." Our win is getting the business and keeping the customer.

A jilted customer
makes revenge a mission.

It's hardly worth any price to have a customer mad at us. He goes out of his way, not just to get even, but to inflict considerably more damage on us than he feels we've caused him.

The problem is typically that the customer feels neglected and disrespected by an impersonal and uncaring business. He assumes, rightly or wrongly, that getting its attention will be difficult, and anticipation of this frustration builds animosity even before he seeks resolution. And because he perceives the enemy as larger than he is, he believes the "justice" he exacts must be multiplied to be felt.

The solution is usually as simple as taking time to show him that our business consists of real people and our people do care about him and his transaction.

Happy customers come and go;
unhappy customers accumulate.

Satisfied customers might do business with us again. We've proven ourselves a trustworthy source, even if only one of many.

Dissatisfied customers have longer memories and look for opportunities to warn others away. They're expensive enemies to have.

It's usually worthwhile to actively look for unhappy customers, open a dialog, and try to make up with them. Often a little attention turns them into equally vocal advocates.

Schaeffer Brothers Piano in Southern California ran regular classified ads offering cash rewards to anyone who could find a dissatisfied Schaeffer customer.

Complaints are signs our customers care and want us to do better.

When a customer complains it often means many others feel the same way but don't bother to tell us—instead they take their business elsewhere. Consequently one complaint represents an opportunity to improve service to many customers.

We should welcome those few who take the initiative to tell us what needs improvement. It's information we vitally need and, although it might not be pleasant to receive it, these customers are going out of their way to help us.

Customers love social causes but they buy value.

"Buy American." "Boycott companies that underpay laborers." "Buy from companies that protect the environment." "Support our local businesses."

Everyone empathizes with a good cause. But when it comes to our money, there's a cause we hold dearer: getting the best value.

Many social causes deserve our support—indeed our survival may even depend on them. But ultimately the decision whether or not to support them is the consumer's, not the retailer's. If we attempt to choose for our customers, they'll simply follow their preferences elsewhere.

> Despite Wal-Mart's extraordinary success in retailing, bad publicity regularly haunts them for sourcing from low-wage areas, lopsided price negotiating with suppliers, displacement of local retailers, etc. As a society we're torn between the social effects of their price efficiency and the savings they bring us as consumers.
>
> Regardless of the often-expressed social concerns, Wal-Mart remains the world's leading retailer. We disdain the killing but we eat the meat.

"I know you have to make a profit; I just don't want you to make it on me."

This is often said with a smile, but not really in jest. It doesn't occur to them that they're really saying, "I'd like you to do some work for me, but I don't want to pay you for it. Put it on the next guy's bill."

Despite the vague understanding that a store sells its merchandise for more than it paid for it, few outside of retailing comprehend and accept the need for this. Profit is regarded more as a windfall to a business than a necessity, finagled rather than earned, and something to be resisted by every savvy consumer.

A sales presentation is not the place to give a business education.

Understanding is the key to relationships. However, most customers' understanding of business is so limited that any discussion of it is counterproductive. It raises so many new questions that the relationship goes backward instead of forward.

Explaining wholesale costs is almost never an effective price-negotiating technique. Although most customers recognize that merchandise has a wholesale cost, they aren't always convinced that a sale must cover it, and few indeed comprehend the breadth of expenses that a store incurs or the need for each sale to contribute to them.

In most cases we do best listening thoroughly to our customer's expectations and exploring for an option acceptable to both parties. It's not necessary for the customer to understand our side to be happy with his.

A lady who sold us a used trumpet got seller's remorse and came back to demand her trumpet back.

In an accusatory tone she told me that she knew we were going to sell her trumpet for more than we had given her. When I agreed she froze. It seemed she had prepared an elaborate argument to expose the fact that we were making a profit on our sales.

I offered to give her the trumpet back and we discussed what she could probably sell it for and what efforts it would require. She decided she was better off selling it to us.

I doubt she'll ever be comfortable with us making a profit on her transaction, but she did assess, correctly I believe, how she would come out best.

A businessman who matches the stereotype has no customers.

TV and movies portray businessmen as ruthless and untrustworthy. A less savvy person attempting to deal with them is sure to get burned.

The stereotype is particularly ironic considering that every experienced businessman has learned the value and necessity of customer satisfaction and on-going relationships. A lopsided deal is more costly for the retailer than the customer since any further business becomes unlikely. No market is so large that unethical transactions don't come back to haunt their purveyors.

Business people who abuse their partners and customers soon run out of people to do business with.

> "Many persons have an idea that one cannot be in business and lead an upright life, whereas the truth is that no one succeeds in business to any great extent who misleads and misrepresents."
>
> **—John Wannamaker**

A low price won't excuse us from service and problems.

No matter how good a price we give an old friend, a relative, or a tough customer, we'll still be expected to take care of any problems, defects, and unforeseen labor and expenses that arise.

Our customer doesn't consider that the low price they paid us included little or nothing to cover problems— they paid us for the product and they look to us to solve the problems.

A sale that doesn't include some profit as insurance against such eventualities doesn't cover its costs. (It's not necessary to include enough in each sale to cover every possible problem—only that every sale contributes to an "insurance fund" that, in sum, is sufficient to cover the problems that occasionally but inevitably arise.)

"Take it back where you bought it" only alienates the nearly converted.

When a customer asks us for help with a product he purchased elsewhere, especially from a troublesome competitor, it's tempting to rub his "mistake" in. "Why don't you take it back to them?" "Don't they know how to operate it?" "Can't they fix it?" "Now you see why their price is lower."

The previous deal is done. At issue now is who gets the next one. They're coming to us because they're unhappy with the competitor's transaction. Do we really want to send them back?

Every customer believes
his neighborhood could support a store.

One of the most common suggestions customers give retailers is to open a store closer to them. To make the case they tell us how much they and their friends buy, how many potential customers are in the market, how the community is growing, and how underserved it is currently.

It's nice to be wanted. And it's not impossible that a customer might point out a market we hadn't noticed. But most proposed markets, despite customers' assurances to the contrary, wouldn't come close to supporting a store. (When they suggest opening a store they don't mean a smaller version proportionate to their community; they'd likely drive right by it to a better selection. They mean a store like the one they're standing in.)

Such suggestions can be acknowledged as the compliments they are. "I'm flattered that you would want us there. Thank you for the suggestion." Anything further can be counterproductive.

One of the best feedback mechanisms we've used in our school band department is a "board of directors." A group of 5-6 band directors is invited to a special lunch with the head of the band department. They discuss our service, instruments, rental and sale plans, repair shop, product selection, special ordering, educational events, promotions, and any other aspects of the store they or we would like to talk about.

They tell us what our competitors are doing, how we stack up against them, and where our strengths and weaknesses are; they make lots of suggestions of how we could be more effective and helpful. Many outstanding ideas and opportunities have originated in these meetings.

Each director gets a check for "travel expense" and is given a gift for participation. We make a big deal of the meeting on our website and social media, and publicize the suggestions and improvements that come from it.

SYSTEMS

Service is dependable only when it follows a system.

A system is a method or routine we adhere to in operating our stores: reconciling the cash, reordering merchandise, counting change, taking messages, scheduling deliveries, taking inventory, approving credit, transferring calls …. Whether by trial and error or forethought, we find and settle on systems that work for us.

When we stay within our systems, we're reasonably reliable and efficient. But when someone doesn't follow the system or we take on a task for which we don't have a system, we make mistakes, miss opportunities, waste resources and effort, and let our customers down.

Good systems aren't the ones
that evolve naturally.

Systems are under constant challenge and assault; users look-ing for shortcuts abbreviate or skip "unnecessary" steps. Occasionally steps should be eliminated, but often "unnec-essary" means only "I don't understand the need for it."

When left to their own evolution and natural rede-sign, systems deteriorate into numerous individual methods—sometimes as many as there are people working—with little communication or coordination between them. In a store, that means information kept precariously on scraps of paper or in memory, sales or work stalling because someone with needed informa-tion is off or unavailable, multiple people doing the same job with conflicting results, chronically inaccurate records—and many mistakes.

A system unwritten
is a system adrift.

In the game of Chinese Whispers, a story is whispered from person to person in a circle. The last person announces what he heard—almost always different enough from the original to provide amusement and amazement.

We often don't notice as our processes are gradually reinterpreted. Only when expensive or embarrassing mistakes come to light do we recall that we once had a system that anticipated and avoided precisely the problem that has arisen. No one remembers changing the system—it just slowly evolved.

Unless systems are written out, only their drifting is dependable.

If the documents are maintained as operating manuals, they can be used for both training and reference. When changes or improvements are intentionally made, the manual is easily updated.

The Roland factory in Japan is one of the most advanced musical instrument factories in the world—spotless, precisely organized, and highly automated.

Its manufacturing processes are thoroughly documented and diagramed on computer screens beside each employee. Steps aren't forgotten, parts aren't confused, tolerances don't drift, and quality checks aren't overlooked. Every product is made according to carefully designed and maintained processes. As a result, Roland instruments are among the most consistent and reliable in the world today.

What's everyone's responsibility is no one's responsibility.

Many tasks of operating a store could be performed by almost anyone on the staff: putting out stock, taking inventory, maintaining signage, arranging merchandise .... Sometimes they're considered general assignments—everyone should use free time between customers to do them.

But jobs that are everyone's responsibility seldom are done well or regularly, and details occasionally ignored soon evolve into lower standards.

Tasks are performed more reliably when they're specifically assigned and become part of someone's daily routine. Yes, everyone should stay busy and there is always something to be done in retail, but it's done better and more reliably when responsibilities are specific.

Every system needs a zealot.

To have a good system, someone must become its advocate, defender, and champion. He must understand the need, be committed to its execution, and ensure that the process is taught, reinforced and followed.

As the system drifts and deteriorates, its champion must diligently seek out those who aren't committed, explain its logic and value, and tirelessly reconvert the unfaithful.

Complex systems impede; simple systems succeed.

If we want a system to be followed, we should make it simple—ideally easier to do correctly than incorrectly.

Scanning a barcode is easier than typing in an item code and price, and far more accurate. Transferring a call to voice mail is easier than writing a message, and more reliable.

We tend to be unrealistically ambitious in system design; we overestimate how many steps a user can remember and how much time he or she will have to execute them. We design forms with information we might need rather than what we can reasonably expect front-line employees to fill in. In the heat of battle our people guess which details are critical and skip the rest. Better to select the necessary details ourselves and require only those.

Like the architect who puts sidewalks where people are going to walk, we have to design systems our people are going to follow.

The school music business requires taking band instruments out to schools for trial and sale. Our salespeople often have hundreds of expensive instruments out at a time. Keeping accurate records of their locations is challenging but vital.

Because the salespeople get early starts when visiting distant schools, they often load their cars with instruments before the rest of the staff arrives.

At one time we asked the salespeople to list the serial numbers of the instruments they took on a note for the inventory manager. You can guess how effective that was, especially when the salespeople were in a hurry.

Eventually we learned to attach two tags to each instrument. The salesman is supposed to peel one tag off and stick it on the clipboard with his name at the top; the inventory manager later scans the tags to the new locations. This is as simple a system as we have so far been able to devise. It has reduced, but certainly not eliminated, inventory tracking problems.

As RFID (Radio Frequency Identification) tags become more feasible, we hope to automate the process. As the instruments and the salesperson go through the door, they'll be scanned automatically.

A business can grow only when its systems can be run by average employees.

Most stores begin with an entrepreneur who has enough retail skills to get the store started. Eventually he hires some "help," while continuing to do most of the critical functions himself. Many stores remain in this stage, occasionally by choice but usually because the entrepreneur can't delegate his responsibilities.

If he wants to grow the business further, he has to break down complex operations into simple processes that can be reliably executed by employees who, although capable, are unlikely to have the same dedication or longevity.

When systems are workable and employees are trained, the business runs smoothly, allowing the entrepreneur time to innovate and the store to grow.

Where mistakes are frequent, processes, not people, are the problem.

A system that seems simple to its designer is often a puzzle to those who must implement it, especially in an environment busy with diverse activities. Those on the frontline seldom have the same experience or understanding of the big picture, and the process is only one of many they have to learn and remember.

More training, better quality people, and increased retention are good prescriptions for almost every problem, but they're expensive and persistent challenges in themselves.

A more user-friendly system is almost always the most efficient remedy for recurring mistakes.

When Wendy's introduced their (delicious) Mandarin Chicken Salad, I had my assistant pick one up for me almost every day for lunch. From the first one a major challenge in their system was apparent—in addition to the pre-packaged salad, the clerk had to gather packages of dressing, noodles, sliced almonds, and a fork/napkin pack—five items in all. A fast food employee rapidly handling orders from a fairly broad menu had predictably little chance of getting it right.

For several months I was amused by the variety of combinations I got. (Amused because they often gave me too many items, and I saved them for when I got too few.) One month I counted: 20 percent left out an item, 30 percent had a wrong item, and 35 percent had too many items; 15 percent of my orders were correct.

74

We've fixed a problem only when we've fixed its source.

When things go wrong we rush to address the problem. A customer is unhappy—we apologize and make it up to him; accounts don't balance—we track down the discrepancy and adjust it; merchandise is out-of stock—we order more; inventory records are inaccurate—we count and correct; displays are disorganized—we straighten them.

We fix the problem but seldom consider why the problem arose—why we offended the customer, why we made the accounting error, why we ran out of stock, why our inventory numbers don't match, or why our displays were left disorganized.

We address the symptoms and ignore the disease. Consequently we deal with these problems again and again. (Insanity is defined as doing the same things over and over and expecting different results.)

A problem isn't fixed until its underlying cause has been fixed.

Toyota uses its "five-why" system to get to root causes.

In *The Toyota Way,* author Jeffrey Liker gives the following example: There's a puddle of oil on the shop floor. Why? Because the machine is leaking. Why? Because the gasket has deteriorated. Why? Because we bought gaskets made of inferior material. Why? Because we chose the lowest cost gaskets. Why? Because the purchasing agent is evaluated on short-term cost savings.

The problem is fixed when the evaluation policy for the purchasing agent is fixed.

The true test of a system is whether the boss can do it.

No deprecation of bosses intended. It's just that as a business grows, a smart boss delegates as much routine as possible to staff. If the systems are designed well, employees handle the functions correctly and consistently and the boss doesn't have to do them. Once the system is proven, the boss rarely has to be involved in the details and he forgets them.

And this makes him an ideal candidate to test whether the system is user-friendly.

There's always a better way.

One of the most creative and gratifying aspects of running a store is improving its processes, especially when the improvement makes the store more efficient, reliable, and profitable.

But such improvement is also a competitive necessity. A retailer who doesn't continually refine his processes, improve his offerings, employ new technologies, and increase his efficiency is quickly passed by competitors. Before long he wonders why what worked for him for so long is no longer profitable.

Procrastination can be friend or foe.

Fighting procrastination is futile. It comes from deep within human nature where what influence we have is weak and temporary. Better to anticipate it and design our systems accordingly.

A liberal return policy helps shoppers overcome the procrastination inherent in making a purchase decision. Then procrastination helps keep the sale sold.

A payroll department avoids begging for employees' hours and commissions by paying the timesheets and commissions turned in by the deadline; stragglers get paid next pay period.

Preliminary reports needing others' approval can be issued with the announcement that they're final unless someone offers corrections before the deadline.

Credit card receipts and documentation are overlooked less often when the cards are in the employees' names and the company reimburses them.

> We once attempted to hire an outstanding salesperson who had just sold his own store. He was interested in our job but couldn't make the decision—he wasn't sure this was what he wanted to do long term, was enjoying his time off, and didn't have pressing financial needs.
>
> After multiple recruiting sessions that seemed to be going nowhere, we finally proposed that he come try it. That non-decision was easier for him and he "tried it" for the rest of his life.

What gets inspected gets done.

Retailing is managing thousands of details. It's virtually impossible to keep up with all of them unless they're put on a list and subjected to regular inspections.

Employees buy into the process when they participate in making the list and setting the criteria. They know first-hand what's important in the operation of their areas.

Living up to the inspection criteria initially takes time and effort, but soon the standards become accepted and maintenance is routine and easy.

The best inspectors are employees.

Having employees rather than management do store inspections sends the psychological message that we're all in agreement on how we want the store to look and operate and are committed to getting it right.

Employee inspectors can also announce results, recognize outstanding efforts, and pass out awards.

In the perennial battle of maintaining our store, we created a program we nicknamed "Neat Police." The staff put together a list of all the routine tasks and requirements: merchandise organized and priced, light bulbs working, boxes off the sales floor, trash picked up on the parking lot, bathrooms clean and stocked, aisles and hallways open, carpets and floors clean, literature available and organized, counters cleared, desks neat, stockrooms organized, break room clean .... Then everyone picked a chore.

My job was picking up the trash on the lawn. I needed the mid-afternoon exercise, and perhaps because I was so visible in this, I never heard a complaint about the tedium or insignificance of anyone else's chore.

Once each day the Neat Policeman does a walk-through inspection. At the weekly sales meeting he presents the scores and gives (or collects) redeemable "Amro bucks." Scores are seldom perfect but I suspect the store is infinitely more organized and ready-to-sell than if we didn't maintain this little game.

DESIGN & DISPLAY

Design and décor
are retail's first impressions.

Before our customers see our products, meet our people, experience our service, or compare our values, they see our stores.

First impressions determine whether we get off to a good start with each new customer or struggle to dispel an unfavorable image. Design and décor are either a solid step forward in the selling process, or an impediment that requires time and effort to overcome.

Décor is marketing too.

The message our décor sends isn't just about organization and cleanliness; it should be a strong statement about selection, quality, pricing, friendliness, dependability, trustworthiness, and professionalism. The message should be consistent with and reinforce the image we're working so hard and spending so much to build.

If the image we want is low prices, perhaps we need sparse décor with simple fixtures, open fluorescent lighting, piled-high displays, plenty of sale signs, and bustle and commotion. But that design works hard against us if the image we want is almost anything else—fashion, leisure fun, reliable performance, trustworthy expertise, safety and security....

We tend to ignore the message our décor sends because we see it every day, but our customers cannot. They have trouble imagining fashion as the latest when our wallpaper is twenty years old, furniture as attractive when it's stored on warehouse shelves, tools as reliable and safe when they're displayed haphazardly, or musical instruments as fun when they're stacked in their cases on shelves.

Design and décor should be a careful and emphatic expression of our marketing message. Straddling the fence or being non-committal not only misses a valuable opportunity, it muddles customers' understanding.

Ignore feasibility and envision the ideal store; then build it.

Forget temporarily all the practical constraints of space, time, money, and personnel, and envision a dream store—ideal inventories, floor pattern, décor, lighting, fixtures, etc. Write out a description, listing all of its features and attractions. Share the concept with employees and brainstorm improvements. Sketch out the floor plan, displays, service areas, signage ....

This, most likely, is the store our customers want and what we and our competitors are moving toward with every small improvement.

Once conceived the vision is irresistible. And the plan is usually more feasible than we think.

Good design requires a designer.

Retailers often believe they have interior design skills; they are almost always painfully mistaken. (Most of us males know too little about interior design to recognize how little we know.) It rarely takes more than walking through the front door of a store to determine whether the retailer or a professional designed it.

Professional designers practice visualization and coordination full-time. They know from experience what makes an effective and attractive design—experience we could get only by making more mistakes than we can afford. They work in the mainstream of trends and materials, have experience with qualities, wear patterns, and deterioration, and are familiar with sources, prices, and availabilities.

Professional design is expensive, no question. Good designers, almost by definition, have expensive tastes. But good design creates an atmosphere and image invaluable to all but the most barebones marketing. (Actually a good designer can help with that image, too.)

Designers working alone create masterpieces of retail impracticality.

Without the retailer's input, designers draw gorgeous stores, often including large open spaces, stylish architectural themes, prominent fixtures and amenities— and far too little focus on the merchandise and activities that must pay for it.

Manufacturers' trendy high-rent showrooms sometimes have multi-story atriums and feature broad staircases, huge murals, exciting A/V, and sparse merchandise. It appears in many cases the manufacturers have too little retail experience to rein in the designers. Whether planned or not, these stores usually end up under promotional expense rather than profit centers.

A good designer solicits, and a good retailer tediously and scrupulously provides, guidance on the store's merchandise requirements and priorities, image and marketing message, customers and habits, and systems and operations.

Form follows function, and selling is the function of a store.

Designers need budgets, retailers need veto power.

A store designer "with good taste" can exceed an unlimited budget. Regardless of the designer's skill and experience, the retailer must be the final arbiter of which elements make financial sense.

Agreeing on a budget is the first step—rarely as simple as it sounds, as both sides are typically stunned by the other's conception of reasonable. Nevertheless it's both more efficient and more pleasant to discuss costs before the designs are begun than after the bids are in.

Good designers provide options and break down costs so the retailer can choose (against anticipated resistance) which features are economically feasible.

You're not in business if you're not in show business.

Potential customers who aren't aware we have what they're looking for drive right by us to a store they believe does. As a result we can't afford to waste any opportunity to show our product in its best light and impress upon customers the breadth and depth of our selection.

Superstores have proven the value of showing a lot of product. Most shoppers are willing to put up with crowds, distant parking, impersonal service, and long lines in exchange for the improved odds of finding what they're looking for.

The essential of good display is making strong, well-planned and favorable impressions of what our stores stock.

Merchandise is for sale, not for storage.

Customers believe what they see is what we've got. Asking insults the virility of half the population—if they don't see it, we don't have it.

Merchandise doesn't sell in a stockroom—it gets ignored, damaged, lost, and stolen. If we have so many products that we can't or don't need to display them all, we probably have too many. We need to tune up our replenishment system and use the freed space and investment to broaden our offerings.

A store with relatively little inventory is bigger to the public than its larger competitors if it has more on display.

When we've made the investment, we should put it out, take credit for it, and let it sell.

Maximize showrooms,
minimize stockrooms.

The theory of selling from a showroom and delivering from a warehouse sounds attractive—the showroom has permanent displays that aren't disrupted and the customer gets fresh in-the-box product.

But theory and reality seldom share perspectives. What's in stock often doesn't match what's on display, frustrating customers and salespeople, and losing sales— because, as every retailer knows, customers always want what we don't have.

When all merchandise is on the sales-floor salespeople sell what they've got, customers choose what's available, and everyone is happy. If it creates a little chaos, that sells, too, since customers are reassured by the activity.

Eliminating stockrooms is usually not only feasible but more efficient. In most cases the only "back room" we need is for receiving—and it should be small enough to prevent storage.

Nothing is beautiful in the wrong light.

Probably the most underrated and unappreciated element of retailing is lighting. Good lighting, strategically directed and focused, can turn slow sellers into bestsellers; dim, flat, misdirected, or unbalanced lighting can doom saleable products to the closeout bin.

Spotlights make all the difference in furniture, car, jewelry, and art showrooms; they bathe high-end products in flattering light, create sparkle and highlights, and draw focus. Carefully selected color temperatures enhance the colors of the merchandise.

(One of the challenges of focused lights is that when merchandise is moved the lights must be refocused—not difficult but often overlooked. One solution is defining display spaces with platforms and other fixed elements where the lights remain focused.)

People like to do business where business is being done.

An empty parking lot, quiet store, idle employees, sparse merchandise, and excess space don't instill confidence. Customers need assurance that they're in the right place, looking at desirable merchandise at attractive prices, and making logical purchase decisions.

Customers, activity, background noise, plentiful merchandise, registers ringing, and a little commotion inspire action.

When customers sense others are buying, they're inclined to buy also.

Deterioration takes no vacation, nor can renovation.

Retailing is a relentless beating for carpet, flooring, wallpaper, paint, woodwork, laminates, display cases, counters, and fixtures. Occasional accidents take major tolls, but everyday wear-and-tear is continuous and persistent. Almost all surfaces are tattered and worn within a few years, and damage or heavy use often makes replacement necessary sooner.

Because most deterioration is gradual we don't notice it as it occurs. We're sometimes surprised and offended when someone suggests our stores need renovating; after all "we just did that a few years ago."

Minor repairs should be part of our regular routine. Paint touch-ups are quick and easy when we save and label the paint from every paint job. Carpet and wallpaper repairs require specialists but can be virtually unnoticeable when we keep excess materials from every renovation. Even laminate chips can be repaired if we request extra materials with fixture orders; buying more later rarely works, as colors change and are discontinued.

SECURITY

There are no new crimes, only new victims.

Stolen credit cards, fraudulent checks, grab and run, smash and grab, concealing merchandise in clothes or bags, hiding in the store until after closing, burglary, robbery—virtually all thefts and frauds are just repetitions thieves commit every day in stores all over the world.

Internal crime includes little innovation as well: pocketing receipts; hiding merchandise in bags, briefcases, and clothing; removing merchandise before or after hours; concealing merchandise in outgoing trash; shipping merchandise to oneself or friends; submitting bogus invoices and receipts for reimbursement; writing checks to oneself; colluding with a vendor for kickbacks; exaggerating payroll hours ....

Fortunately crime isn't creative—just persistent. And so must be crime prevention.

Opportunity makes the thief.

Few crimes are the result of criminal premeditation. Circumstances create them—someone simply notices that merchandise is unguarded, the system has holes, or no one is paying attention.

A little (expensive) experience allows us to spot most crimes before they're committed. We can predict shoplifting from display locations, expense account abuse from reimbursement requirements, inventory theft from handling procedures, embezzlement from accounting processes ....

Crime prevention is a routine.

Heading off most crimes isn't difficult: keep sales floors attended; check customer IDs for checks and credit cards; remove expensive merchandise from display windows overnight; get merchandise off the dock quickly; display expensive items away from doors and within visibility; use clear trash bags and check the dumpster periodically; limit keys and change locks regularly; review bank statements and checks monthly; do sample audits regularly; ask questions to demonstrate attention, etc.

Employee training is the first line of defense.

Employees who know what to look for can prevent a lot of crimes.

Training can be structured teaching and review of the common crimes and their prevention. Or it could be open discussion of ways the store has been taken in the past; long-term employees can relate them from experience, giving the lessons more immediacy and relevance.

We once caught two boys, 14 and 16, trying to sell us stolen cymbals—we knew they were stolen because they were still on our inventory.

The boys confessed to making regular hauls over more than a month. They itemized $2666 worth of drum equipment they had taken, including 18 cymbals. One said he often made trips back and forth to the car to drop off the loot and admitted to stuffing three cymbals in his shirt at once. Not only were we blind, but deaf.

Fortunately they overestimated our incompetence, but apparently not by much.

The best clue is the sale is too easy.

Even the smartest of crooks rarely imitate real customers well. They know too little about the merchandise, don't ask the right questions, spend too little time selecting, and aren't concerned with pricing—they buy too easily.

Purchases of high-priced items by phone, especially from outside our normal market areas, should always be suspect, as should sending a courier to pick up items.

Commissioned salespeople are easy targets for these tactics because they want to believe the sale is legitimate. (Getting credit card approval or bank check verification doesn't mean it won't be returned later as fraudulent—approval means only that there's enough room on the card or money in the account, not that the person using it is its owner.)

An elderly lady once reported to the police that her life savings had been stolen in an investment scam. The investigator asked if the investment didn't seem too good to be true, and the lady admitted that it had. When he asked why she didn't call the police first to see if it was a fraud, she said she was afraid they'd tell her it was.

Security cameras are better prevention than proof.

Security cameras are improving in quality, affordability, and recording time, but their effectiveness is still more perception than reality.

When cameras are placed conspicuously they deter robberies and burglaries, as well as head off shoplifting.

But their usefulness in solving crimes is limited. Even when we can review the crime in action, the picture is usually too small and fuzzy to identify perpetrators, read license plates, or prove the details. The video is just a souvenir of our loss.

> Cameras don't deter much if people don't notice them. The Internet serves up enough security videos of people having sex in public places to threaten the livelihoods of professional pornographers.

Integrated software is internal crime detection and prevention.

Good accounting software makes theft and embezzlement more challenging. The double entries required by an integrated system require that merchandise purchases are added to inventory as well as to payables, that merchandise sold increases the bank balance as the inventory is relieved, that payments on accounts increase the bank balance as the customer balance is decreased, that payments to suppliers reduce accounts payable as the bank balance is decreased ....

Shortages of cash or inventory are detectable when the amounts on hand no longer match their software balances. Hiding such discrepancies would require complex entries made by knowledgeable accounting employees—and even those entries leave a trail.

"Justice" doesn't mean for the victim.

Courts are focused on punishment of the criminal, not compensation of the victim. Prosecution requires making a case, showing up in court (sometimes multiple times), and a great deal of waiting time. Even when restitution is mandated, it seldom makes up for our lost time and trouble.

Our most effective use of the justice system is often only as a threat to recover our merchandise or money. Then we can get back to making a living.

100

Prevention beats prosecution.

Catching a crook isn't really crime solution; it's the beginning of a long and painful process. The legal system is slow, frustrating, and inefficient, and often renders disappointing results.

Will we feel better seeing a perpetrator get his due? A few hours sitting outside the courtroom dampens our satisfaction. Will the world be better off with a crook off the street? He's one of millions in a continually replenished hoard.

Better to discourage criminals from committing their crimes in our stores and let the police catch them—somewhere else.

Here's a story for "Stupid Crooks." A few years ago my brother noticed his inexpensive digital recorder was missing from his desk. He asked around and no one knew anything, so out of curiosity he reviewed the security recordings. He discovered that in the middle of the previous Sunday afternoon an unknown man wandered into his office and pocketed it. He reviewed the recording further to see how this man had gotten in on a day the store was closed.

It turned out we had carpet installed in an area of the store that day. An employee opened the back door and stayed all day with the carpet layers. But the thief wasn't with the carpet layers. The video showed him watching the workmen coming and going through the backdoor and then going in when no one was looking. He stayed just ahead of or behind the workmen and employee, and wandered through several stockrooms and offices totally undetected. At one point he left the store and came back again. Apparently the only things he took fit in his pocket. Finally the employee saw him outside the backdoor and ran him off.

But the story continues. We found a video tape in one of the areas where he'd been. It wasn't a format we could play but the name of a local convenience store was written on it. We took the tape to the store. It was video of our thief burglarizing the convenience store, including taking the tape.

A week later police caught him burglarizing a home. Presumably the two videos made it a little more difficult for him to plead "first offense."

INVENTORY

101

We can't sell what we don't have.

The basic function of retailing is anticipating what products customers will want and making them conveniently available when customers are ready to buy. If we miss at this, nothing else can make up—we're simply out of the game.

Since we can't precisely predict how many of which items will sell and when, we make our best guesses (aided hopefully by historical data and trends). When we guess low, we miss sales; when we guess high, we waste investment that could have been put into other merchandise that would sell.

102

Inventory is marketing too.

An academic once observed (profoundly, apparently), "Inventory is the price a business pays for lack of information." In other words, if we knew exactly what we were going to sell and when, we would stock only those products and only at the precise times they were needed. Shelves wouldn't be needed as they'd be empty.

Perhaps that's true in a manufacturing or warehouse business, but it doesn't work in retail.

The breadth and depth of a store's inventory makes a strong marketing statement to retail customers. Their impression of it on one visit determines whether they'll return later for a different need. In addition some customers won't make a purchase until they've seen their options—and they shop where they believe those options are available.

Success in retail depends on having inventory. Inventory capital should be invested wisely—but wisely doesn't mean minimizing inventory.

A store is not a store without inventory.

103

Customers want choices, even when the choice is clear.

Stocking just the big sellers seems a logical and efficient strategy. But big sellers often aren't big sellers when there's nothing for customers to compare them to.

Shoppers want selections. They want to consider differences, compare prices, and determine for themselves which products best meet their needs. The more significant the purchase, the more thoroughly they want to compare.

We can have exactly the product they need and will eventually buy, and be able to explain why, but unless it's a minor purchase they won't buy it until they've seen for themselves what else is available.

This means we occasionally have to stock products more for comparisons than for expected sales. We don't need every product on the market—too many choices confuse shoppers. In most cases a product on each side of the big seller is appropriate, as most shoppers are skeptical of the least expensive and believe they don't need the most expensive.

104

No inventory is ever enough.

Normal people dream about tropical islands and sexy partners. Retailers dream about the stores we could build, the selections we could offer, the customers we could satisfy, the sales we could achieve—if only we could afford more inventory. Like the rabbit at the greyhound track, the investment we "need" is always just beyond our reach.

Unfortunately, as we tell our sadly underprivileged kids, we have to learn to live within our means. That means choosing carefully (and painfully) the items that offer our companies the best return and the best fit with our marketing strategy.

105

Love your products, but only for their sales.

We should get to know our products well, use them whenever we can, recognize and appreciate their benefits, believe in them, and talk them up. But we should love them only as merchandise.

Many of us were attracted to our areas of retail by the products. Sometimes they were part of a hobby that has long fascinated us or a field we've accumulated expertise in. Knowledge and experience create affinity.

But our personal attractions should not influence our merchandise selection. We're stocking a store, not a recreation center or museum.

Best is seldom best seller. Our customers' uses are often not the same as ours, and customers are rarely as infatuated with the product as we are.

106

Taking inventory isn't just a tax obligation.

Good retailers track and verify inventory continuously, turning up discrepancies, shrinkage, overstocks, and stock-outs quickly for fast resolution. Accurate inventory records improve security, facilitate more efficient and precise reordering, allow faster recognition of trends, and enable correct and timely financial statements.

Cycle counting is taking inventory in segments on a regular schedule. Because inventories are confirmed and corrected continuously, records are reliable throughout the year and there are no year-end surprises.

107

"Maximize turnover" is foolish advice.

Many consultants chant a mantra of "maximize turnover," apparently unaware of how silly such a recommendation is.

If we want to increase our turnover, we can simply eliminate the 50 percent of our inventory with the lowest turnover. If we want it even higher, we can do it again. We can make our turnover almost anything we want it to be. What's left of our sales might no longer support our business, but our ratios will be the envy of the industry.

Turnover is not the goal—profit is. We should invest every dollar we have reasonable access to in the inventory that will offer us the best (net) profit. What that does to our turnover ratio is irrelevant.

(This doesn't mean turnover ratios are totally useless—only that they're grossly misused and a major distraction. Low turnover sometimes indicates dead stock, and high turnover sometimes indicates too little stock. (However, most retailers suffer from a blend of the two that renders their overall turnover ratios meaningless.)

108

Inventory expands to fill all space.

There's never enough space for the merchandise we want to keep. Whatever we have, there's always more we could sell if only we had a place to put it.

When a hole appears on a sales floor or shelf, it fills quickly, although rarely with the correct items. Attractive displays turn into stacks and piles. Spacious aisles become narrow paths, shelves and bins are loaded far beyond capacity, categories blur and overlap, and few products get the displays they deserve.

When new merchandise arrives, finding a place for it is a battle. Docks turn into permanent storage, and offices, hallways, bathrooms, and elevators become fair game.

In the public markets in China vendors rent small booths they cram full of their niche merchandise—chickens, fish, turtles, eels, woks, spices, pearls, jewelry, crafts, fabrics, clothes, pirated videos, knock-off watches—anything the Chinese or their tourists could want.

I felt an immediate affinity for one t-shirt vendor, surrounded in his tiny booth by mammoth stacks of t-shirts in every color, style, and clever saying, piled high above his head to the rafters. When I agreed to buy one if he had it in my size, he climbed up his ladder, tunneled through the stacks, and emerged with the prize without any hint of pride in his accomplishment. If he had set off an avalanche we might still be digging for him.

The show was worth much more than the shirt. I brought the picture and story home to our staff as it epitomized not only our daily challenge with inventory and storage but the value of organization and efficiency.

Enough space isn't the solution, and sometimes is the problem.

Our first reaction to a crowded store is that we need more room. Such logic recalls Dizzy Dean's suggestion of moving first base back five feet to avoid close calls. We'd just fill the new area with a bigger jumble of merchandise and enlarge the mess. (Space limitations are the only inventory controls some of us have.)

An abundance of space indulges our tendencies to disorganization. We accumulate merchandise we don't need, become comfortable with our dead stock, and can't find products we might otherwise sell.

What we need isn't more space, but purchase planning, inventory management, and discipline. Ideally we should analyze which products provide the best net profit, allocate our space accordingly, quickly move out the dead and less desirable pieces, and stick like Prussian soldiers to the battle plan.

Efficiency is seldom fun but always rewarding.

110

Outside storage is an addiction.

Self-storage is a brilliant business concept—if it doesn't consume us all like a fast-growing cancer.

Storage facilities are easy to accumulate and difficult to shed. The space inevitably fills up with things "we might need someday"—dead merchandise, old fixtures, outdated paperwork ....

Few wholesale purchases are good enough to offset the added expense of facility rental, tracking, moving, insurance, deterioration, capital investment, etc. If we don't need it on the sales floor, we probably don't need it.

As for the old fixtures, it's almost always cheaper to throw them away, save the storage expense, and buy new ones if we ever really need them. Yes, they were expensive—and they'll be more expensive after we store them.

PURCHASING

111

Profits are easier made in buying than selling.

Making additional profit selling requires finding more customers—often difficult and expensive. Improving profits by reducing expenses means doing without something we feel we need. But additional profit in purchasing is often a simple matter of asking the right question or proposing the right agreement.

With net margins typically 1-3 percent of revenues, purchasing can easily be the difference between profit and loss.

Purchasing at many small stores goes something like this: A supplier's representative calls. After some small talk, the rep asks what merchandise the store needs. The buyer, who doubles as a salesperson, remembers the customer he disappointed this morning. "Yeah, glad you asked," he says. "We need some LaVoz MH tenor sax reeds; I missed a sale this morning for some. Sure, six boxes ought to do it. And let's see ... Hey, Mike. Can you think of anything we need from East Coast Wholesale? Yeah, that's right— we're out of ProMark 7ANs, and we could use some Hohner Blues Harps in G, too. Yeah, a dozen of each is good. And let's see ... I guess that's about it for now. Yeah, just put my name down for the purchase order number. OK, thanks for calling, Tom. Talk to you next week."

What's wrong with this scenario? Lots! Products are ordered after stock runs out and sales are missed; it's highly unlikely that all needed products are ordered; no checking to see what's already on order; quantities are anything but calculated; there's no negotiation of wholesale prices or terms—the vendor who calls or comes by gets the order; no consideration of the vendor's fill/back-order rate; no purchase order was issued/no record of the order was made. For starters.

112

A good salesman makes a bad buyer.

Logic tells us our salespeople could be great buyers. They know the products, know firsthand what customers are asking for and are willing to pay, and are experienced negotiators.

Yet good salespeople are usually terrible choices for buyers. Their empathy with salesmen makes them reluctant to send anyone away without an order. Their social personalities are alien to detail—they lack the patience to maintain and study inventory records, calculate returns, project future sales and reorder points, maintain purchase order records, and process invoices.

But why distract a good salesman with order duties anyway? They're too rare and valuable to take them away from customers.

113

Wholesale is the asking price and the highest any retailer pays.

Wholesale is the price the supplier would like the retailer to pay. But for a sale to take place both buyer and seller must agree on a price.

Experienced suppliers aren't offended by price negotiation; they recognize its potential to create a mutually profitable deal and regret it when a buyer doesn't try to make a purchase possible.

Negotiations can be friendly, polite, and pleasant—not one against another, but rather two looking together for a way to structure a sale that works for both.

114

Better pricing takes many guises.

A supplier's market is rarely easier than a retailer's; they too have to hustle and scrap for new customers and added sales. Most keep a few closing concessions handy to throw in when needed to get an order. Often it's an extra discount, an introductory price, or some special-situation merchandise.

When a vendor insists there is only one price for his products, he often maintains flexibility in other aspects of the sale: extended terms, free freight, return options, mark-down money, promotional products, giveaways, displays, etc.

Advertising co-op is a popular technique that "one-price" suppliers use to give extra discounts. The terms for claiming it can be extremely loose—sometimes it's simply deducted as a percent of each purchase.

Some years ago CompUSA got into an accounting and stockholder flap that caused a precipitous drop in their stock price. Their financial statements showed they billed and collected from their suppliers $4 mil in advertising co-op while spending only about $1 mil on advertising. Investors complained that previously reported profits were not really profits on sales as reported but rather on overbilling, possibly fraudulently, their suppliers for advertising.

When the Wall Street Journal contacted IBM, Apple, Compaq, and Hewlett-Packard, none would comment other than to praise the company's marketing and high sales. None of them appeared interested in pursuing the "overbilled" advertising money.

Did these companies really allow themselves to be defrauded of almost $3 mil? Advertising is easily documented with media invoices, newspaper tear-outs, and audio and video files. Or was this four manufacturers' way of allowing extra discounts to a large, hard-bargaining retailer without selling at "off the card" prices?

115

Reorder is a job for computers.

We can't sell it if we don't have it, and computer software is the most effective, reliable, and efficient way to ensure we have it.

Looking around for what's low and "Tell me what you sold," hardly qualify as business systems. We'd miss sales due to stock-outs and stock more of many items than we need. Making hand counts before each order is feasible only for the smallest of inventories. Few markets will forgive such inefficiencies.

Good business software keeps track of what we have and what we've sold. From these we can calculate and set the quantities we want to stock. The automatic reorder function creates recommended purchase orders calculated by comparing inventory on hand to the ideal quantities we set.

Such a system can track thousands of SKUs continuously, without forgetting or overlooking any of them.

116

Computerizing inventory doesn't require closing the business.

Setting up perpetual inventory need not be painful. Rather than trying to enter all inventory at once, enter it as it's replaced.

When items are ordered, create their computer records for the purchase order. When the items arrive, receive them through the computer. At the register if the item has been entered, scan it; if it hasn't, ring it up by the old method.

Within a few months all good-selling products will be on inventory. (Items that aren't might need closing out rather than entering.)

117

Country of origin is a choice for consumers, not retailers.

Some people feel we should "keep our money at home," "buy American," "support American workers," ....

Whether their economic philosophy is right or wrong is not for us to decide; as retailers, we have a market-imposed responsibility to offer the products our customers want.

Proposing that stores take the choice out of consumers' hands is naïve and contrary to democratic principles.

The slogans and their sentiments strike a chord with many people, and some retailers play off them; customers will determine its effectiveness. Typically most consumers prove more interested in value for their money.

118

Brand names are shoppers' substitutes for research.

Most consumers don't have the time or the information to make objective comparisons of products. They use brand names as a shortcut, and are willing to pay more for names they recognize and trust.

A manufacturer who creates recognition and a reputation for his product increases both demand for his product and the price it will bring. Companies like Nike, Callaway, David Yurman, and Tommy Hilfiger have found their products will sell for prices virtually unrelated to their costs of production and limited only by the reputations they can build.

Retailers with name brand products benefit from the increased demand and sometimes from the higher prices, but also from the credibility of offering products consumers trust and want.

119

Choose a brand like you choose a wife.

Taking on a major brand is a serious commitment. It requires dedicated capital, appropriate display space, sales training, time for salespeople to build confidence, advertising to create a reputation in the market for having it ....

Changing brands is seldom as simple as sending purchase orders to a different address. Consumers expect consistency in a retailer's products; a company that pushes one brand today and another tomorrow loses credibility. Customers' brand loyalties can be changed but it's usually a slow process. And customers who bought products previously expect ongoing support for them.

120

It's a marriage, but seldom made in heaven.

Retailers need saleable products from reliable manufacturers. Manufacturers need active retailers to show and sell their products. Neither can survive without the other. Yet the relationship is anything but easy and not always happy.

Retailers complain that manufacturers sell through too many outlets, have unreasonable order expectations, set their wholesales too high and their MSRPs and MAPs too low, don't offer enough advertising support, and can't deliver quickly enough. (A partial list, to be sure.)

Manufacturers complain that dealers don't stock their products adequately, display them improperly, don't know the products, stock too many competitive products, don't implement their marketing plans, don't use their in-store promotional materials, don't advertise enough, and don't pay their bills on time. (Our manufacturer friends could extend this list.)

121

Manufacturers and retailers wear different glasses.

A manufacturer's understanding of a retailer's challenges is typically woefully limited. He doesn't maintain retail space, entertain shoppers, fight price wars, negotiate consumer prices, arrange financing, or deal with individual users' problems—indeed he seldom faces the end-user directly. From a manufacturer's perspective, "making a sale" means to a retailer. What happens to the product after that is not part of his daily world.

But, in fairness, our understanding of the manufacturer's business is also lacking. We know little of R&D, product design, patents, parts sourcing, production, packaging, national advertising, tradeshow exhibits, distribution channels, dealer credit, traveling reps ....

The predictable result of these differences in perspective is occasional misunderstanding and frustration.

This marriage lasts
until a better one comes along.

A manufacturer/retailer relationship exists only as long as both parties feel it's the best available to them. A manufacturer continues selling to his current dealer until he finds a more profitable alternative dealer. A dealer continues to sell the manufacturer's product until he finds a more profitable alternative product.

Despite seeing this in action throughout our careers, its callousness still occasionally surprises us. Nevertheless, it's better to recognize and plan for life's realities than to be caught completely off-guard.

In 2007 the Eagles broke all precedents and shocked the record business by releasing their new CD "Long Road out of Eden" exclusively through Wal-Mart, cutting record labels and record stores completely out of the chain.

Eagles manager Irving Azoff said the decision was simple: "Do you want to make pennies (per CD) (through traditional channels) or do you want to make dollars from Wal-Mart?"

Such an end-run was incomprehensible to traditional record stores, even as it occurred.

(Wal-Mart reportedly sold 3.2 million copies netting the Eagles $50 million, compared to ~$10 million traditional channels might have netted.)

123

Don't take it personally; it's just business for you too.

We're offended when a longtime vendor abandons us for a competitor. We "can't believe they'd do it to us, especially considering" how many years we've been a dealer, what we've done to build the line, how long we've known them, how hard we've worked for them ....

Despite the familiarity that occasionally develops, vendor relationships shouldn't be mistaken for personal loyalties. (If you doubt this, consider how often you'd get a call or a card from a vendor if either of you changed occupations.)

Ultimately vendors have to do what's best for their businesses. If a competitor can place bigger orders, in most cases he'll get the line.

But is that really so different from what we do when a more profitable line becomes available?

124

Building a brand doesn't make you its owner.

As retailers we feel it's our grass roots efforts that build a brand in our markets. By advertising, promoting, displaying, demonstrating, and talking up a brand we become heavily invested in it; it often becomes part of our identities. When the manufacturer broadens or changes distribution, we feel double-crossed and cheated, as if something we created has been stolen from us.

Building a brand owned by someone else is inherently risky—the brand owner can move it whenever he feels it's advantageous, transferring all the fruits of our efforts to our new competitor.

As a result some retailers say a store's advertising and promotion should be focused on the store, not the product.

I couldn't count how many manufacturers have come to us with new or relatively unknown products they want us to introduce in our market. Their pitch is typically, "It's a great product at a low price, and you can make high margins because there are no other dealers for it."

We know we can build a local market for most products; we've done it many times. But we also know that once demand increases—due largely to efforts of dealers like us—competitors, including Internet discounters, will request the line and the manufacturer will likely welcome them. The unknown brand that we adopted, built, and were forced to abandon just as it began to sell well will then be our competitors'.

If we have a long-term, stable and trusted vendor, we think it's more in our interests to support his brand than to introduce a new and unpredictable brand to our market.

125

Beholden to one brand is precarious business.

In investing, putting all your eggs in one basket is risky. Occasionally the outcome is a home run, but too often it's disaster.

The risks with one brand aren't much better. A manufacturer's products can become outdated or overpriced, strikes can delay or prevent production, distribution can be broadened beyond retail profitability, distribution channels can be changed, important products and lines can be abandoned, the company can get into financial or legal trouble, or management can just become unreasonable to work with.

Saleable, profitable products are essential, but being locked into a single source and brand is full of hazards.

126

The price premium a brand name commands belongs to the brand owner.

Consumers are willing to pay more for brands they know and trust. However the beneficiary of the higher price is seldom the retailer; the full value of the brand is usually extracted by the brand's owner through higher wholesale pricing and broadened distribution.

Some brands have such strong demand that, despite highly saturated distribution, retailers feel they can't afford to be without them (e.g., Coca-Cola, Canon, Budweiser, Callaway). Wholesale prices are often high but retail pricing is typically too competitive for any but the most efficient retailers to make a profit.

(In these cases many small retailers stock the name brand but promote alternatives. The high-demand products are put on display and priced competitively, and alternative products are attractively displayed and priced nearby with salespeople well trained in explaining their benefits. The scenario is predictable, as is its loathing by name brand manufacturers.)

Many car manufacturers open enough dealerships in each market to ensure that their dealers don't make more than minimum margins on their sales; dealers often say they rely on their service departments to keep their businesses afloat.

Franchised hotels and fast-food restaurants often complain that when they become profitable the franchisors open more outlets around them.

In the music products industry, as in many others, when a product or brand achieves dominance, the manufacturer often raises the wholesale, reduces MSRP, and opens more retailers or Internet outlets.

127

The rookie mistake of purchasing is wanting every product and line.

New salespeople often believe if they had every brand they could make every sale.

Before making a large purchase, shoppers typically visit several stores. Competitive stores naturally show products the other stores don't have. When a shopper tells us he's considering a competitive product, it's usually because a competitive store has shown it to him. If we had that product, the competitor would be showing—and customers would be requesting—another product we don't have.

If all stores carried all products, all sales would be price wars—no retailer would be profitable and no manufacturer would have focused representation.

Better to choose lines carefully, stock them adequately, learn them thoroughly, and show them well. Then may the best store win—profitably.

128

Manufacturers claim adding a dealer stimulates sales; retailers say it splits the pie.

Few would expect more groceries or gas to be sold because another grocery store or gas station comes to town, but perhaps it's possible with more discretionary products.

Evidence from both sides is mostly anecdotal and virtually always biased.

In most cases when a large new competitor enters a market, the existing stores see a reduction in sales and often in gross margins; whether total sales increase usually depends on whether total advertising and promotion increase. When a strong competitor leaves a market, the remaining dealers typically pick up business—but in many cases not enough to keep total market sales at previous levels.

Although most retailers dismiss as ridiculous the contention that adding dealers could increase their sales, the scenario is not impossible.

In the home organ business in the 1970s dealers demonstrating organs at fairs and malls created customers who then sometimes comparison-shopped with competing dealers. The non-promoting dealers would probably (reluctantly) admit that they would have sold few organs without someone else getting out and stirring up interest. The home organ market was virtually nonexistent until some energetic and enterprising dealers exposed the public to the product.

129

The desirability of a product isn't market demand, but profitability.

How many we can sell is of little interest if they don't sell at a profit (a net profit, not just a gross profit).

When gross margins are too small or the expenses of the sale too high, selling more isn't a bonus but a burden. If too many dealers are selling the same products in a market, none of them will make a reasonable return on efforts and investment.

Customers making large purchases often take advantage of a dealer's showroom, displays, inventory investment, salespeople, and expertise, and then buy from a lower-price dealer whose expenses don't include these things. (Customers don't think of this as unethical—they perceive it as a free-market opportunity they have a personal duty to take advantage of.)

A product has potential for a retailer only when pricing and distribution allow a reasonable profit.

130

Manufacturers limit distribution when it increases sales.

Most manufacturers recognize that when they have too many dealers in a market, the dealers stop promoting their products and eventually drop their lines. Consequently manufacturers restrict their distribution to the degree necessary to attract dealers and keep them interested. Carefully managing the balance maximizes a manufacturer's sales.

Retailers shouldn't interpret a manufacturer's limited distribution policy as anything but a profit-maximization strategy. Manufacturers run businesses; even when they enjoy business friendships, their ultimate responsibility is to make their businesses survive and prosper.

131

Limited distribution is popular marketing for products with limited demand.

Dealer exclusivity is an especially effective strategy for manufacturers with small market shares; they have few dealers anyway and it's tough for them to attract new ones unless they can offer the promise of enhanced profitability.

Unfortunately when market demand increases it makes economic sense for the manufacturer to broaden distribution. The original retailers, of course, complain that they created the local market for the product and then the manufacturer took away its profitability by adding or changing dealers. It's easy to sympathize with their recurring struggle—but not their failure to anticipate the recurring outcome.

132

The brand you build could be your own.

One method of ensuring that our effort and investment in building a brand accrue to us and not our competitors is creating our own brand.

Many manufacturers are happy to make products for retailers to our or their specifications. Indeed many of the top brand name products are made by contract manufacturers who would gladly make similar products for us. The global market and off-shore manufacturing have made it easier than ever to find manufacturers and products for store branding.

Because contract manufacturers know the brand owner could have other factories make the product, their pricing stays competitive—often surprisingly below the wholesales of similar name brand products.

Cutting out the supplier means doing his work.

Going direct to the source sounds like a simple, logical, and profitable step for a retailer. Unfortunately it involves much more than just finding willing manufacturers.

We assume for ourselves all the work the supplier typically does—designing products and packaging; creating and registering names and trademarks; negotiating manufacturing prices, quantities, and deliveries (lead times are typically long and fill-in orders aren't quickly available): assuring quality; arranging shipping (usually from overseas); navigating customs; dealing with discrepancies and defects; promoting the brand; handling and absorbing warranty problems; ....

Often these steps make more economic sense when their costs are spread over multiple retailers' orders—which is what a supplier does. Unless the quantities are substantial or there are strong strategic reasons for owning the brand, it often makes more sense to focus on retailing and let the supplier do his job.

134

All manufacturers fear dependency on dominant retailers but few can resist their orders.

We don't really have to remind manufacturers of the pitfalls of becoming dependent on one or several large retailers—they're acutely aware.

Yet the economics of manufacturing—spreading fixed costs of design, development, machinery, and set-up over larger production—make the temptation of higher sales more than most manufacturers can resist.

An informal scan of stores in any market confirms that, with few exceptions, larger stores and chains get the top brands. Most manufacturers privately admit to being uneasy with their precarious situations but say they have little choice.

135

Manufacturing and retailing are separate skills, rarely combined successfully.

The frustrations of dealing with independent and often contrary retailers cause many manufacturers to dream of operating their own stores. They would, at last, be able to display, market, and merchandise their products as they feel the products deserve. And if the stores merely break even, they reason, increased product sales would still make the effort worthwhile.

But most manufacturers who have ventured into retailing have found it far more difficult than they expected. They discover that retailing's many details require dedicated focus and experience—and take time, energy, and resources away from manufacturing.

Most manufacturers who try retailing retreat to what they do well, and leave the retailing to those who specialize in it.

136

Direct distribution is retailing too.

It seems simple enough to put up a website, take orders and ship products. Why does a manufacturer need a retailer to do that?

Because simple is seldom as simple as simple seems. Customers have questions, need information, want to see and try the product, need expert advice, require financing .... Fraud must be detected, returns processed, defective products repaired or replaced, unhappy customers pacified ....

True, some sales are as easy as charging a credit card and printing a shipping label, but these are rare and usually highly competitive and marginally profitable. The rest are retail in all its complexities, regardless of the medium.

There's little reason for any manufacturer to distribute his own products, on the Internet or elsewhere; there are too many good retailers bidding to do it more efficiently.

137

A struggling manufacturer spreads the pain.

The troubles of a competitive manufacturer are no cause for celebration as the distress is highly contagious.

A manufacturer in crisis must take urgent and sometimes reckless action to save his business, and the fallout is seldom confined to his own company.

Short-term cash needs often force a manufacturer to liquidate inventories, usually by temporarily reducing wholesales or broadening his distribution network. Adding dealers upsets the established distribution, precipitating dealer complaints and setting off brand shifting.

As retailers who buy at the reduced wholesales begin to advertise and sell below previous market prices, dealer complaints accumulate; complaints are especially vehement when the new market price is below the previous wholesale. Dealers who paid the old price feel cheated; the manufacturer either pacifies them with retroactive discounts or risks losing their representation in the future.

Competitive manufacturers, feeling the pinch of both the new lower prices and lost sales to the liquidation, face pressure to maintain production and market share. So they reduce their own pricing, sometimes beyond sustainability.

Customers who bought any of the products at previous prices are unhappy with both manufacturer and retailer. No one is sure what the real value of the products is. The new lower prices become the new standards and both customer and retailer become hesitant to buy at prices that reflect the true costs of production.

VENDOR REPS

138

A rep is a bridge over the abyss between manufacturer and retailer.

Manufacturers and retailers live in different worlds. A manufacturer knows little of retail locations, display, salesmanship, advertising, and the myriad other challenges and expenses a retailer faces. Likewise a retailer knows little of product development, patents, sourcing, factories, quality control, distribution, and other manufacturing necessities.

The rep is the assigned interface between the two disparate factions, charged with forging and maintaining mutually profitable relationships. He brings the manufacturer's offerings and messages to the retailer, and encourages and facilitates transactions. Smart manufacturers rely on the rep to bring back market feedback and suggest ways products and business could be improved.

Buying sometimes
requires salesmanship too.

Attracting a manufacturer away from an existing relationship or convincing him to broaden distribution often requires going on the offensive—we have to pursue the line and convince the rep his sales will increase by opening us as a dealer.

A rep tends to judge our potential largely from superficial aspects of our stores—size, products, amount of inventory, design, décor, displays, organization, customer traffic ....

But we can provide other information too, often more influential. We can tout our sales, play up our promotions and events, explain our customer followings, brag about recent transactions, talk up our credit history, point out our long-term stability, show off our systems, introduce impressive salespeople, give a tour of our facilities, etc.

"Business has been great; we can hardly keep up." "We've sold six of these already this week." "We're the biggest dealer in the area for ...." "We get a lot of requests for products like yours." "Let me show you around and introduce some of our people." "Things are a little disorganized because we just finished a huge sale."

Credit history and financial strength strike a particularly strong chord with many reps who are continually frustrated by dealers who don't pass credit approval, are put on credit-hold, or impose buying freezes because they're out of cash.

We created a store tour that we often give to important potential customers, but sometimes also to reps of lines we want.

Key people give short presentations of their areas: the band manager tells how many full-time salespeople we have in the field and how many schools we call on per week; the accessory manager shows his large inventory, sophisticated inventory tracking, and automatic-reorder process; the repair shop manager tells how many repair techs he has, their total years of experience, the number of instruments they repair per week, and their average turn-around time; the piano manager introduces experienced salespeople and shows some of the expensive products we sell; the print music manager tells how many pieces of music we stock and demonstrates software we created to locate requested songs among the thousands of song books.

When the tour is over the rep is usually ready to do business.

A friend once pointed out that establishing a new brand relationship involves all the intrigue of a new romance:

- Both sides size each other up for desirability.
- Both are elusive concerning their desire for a relationship lest their eagerness scare off the potential partner.
- Questions aren't overt but judgments are constant.
- Appearance, financial means, reliability, integrity, and ability to produce are prime criteria.
- Both are (usually) looking for a long-term relationship.
- Both carefully weigh their other options before making commitments.

140

Distribution is determined by the market, not vendor benevolence.

Manufacturers want the broadest possible distribution of their products to maximize their sales and profits. Retailers want the narrowest possible distribution of the manufacturer's products to maximize their own sales and profits. The compromise they reach depends almost exclusively on the relative market strengths of the product and the dealer.

If the product is such a hot seller that dealers would be unwise to do without it regardless of how many dealers are in a market, distribution will probably not be limited at all (except possibly by the rep's and the manufacturer's desire not to have to deal with small orders and dealers). If, on the other hand, the product is a slow seller, the rep might be lucky to get just one dealer in a market to handle it; exclusive distribution is often a given.

The clout of the dealer is determined by how much of the product he can sell in the market. If he can sell large quantities, the rep might feel that he wouldn't get the same sales from any single or combination of alternative outlets in the market. Rather than risk upsetting or losing the good dealer, he'll limit his distribution in this market to the large dealer.

If, on the other hand, a dealer's sales are low, the rep can be expected to open additional outlets if he can or change to a dealer that offers more promise; if the existing small dealer becomes upset, he hasn't lost much.

A jilted dealer is sometimes surprised by a manufacturer's assessment of better potential elsewhere, but he should not be surprised by the process.

Schedule and agenda
are the buyer's to set.

Many retailers feel obligated to accept and entertain manufacturer reps according to the rep's timetable and plan. Experienced retailers usually take control of their time and plan their own agendas.

"We're happy to have you here and looking forward to a long and mutually profitable relationship. Let's talk about how we can best work together.

"Please let me know in advance when you're coming and I will reserve some time and gather my information.

"Our uninterrupted time is likely to be brief so we'll need to stay focused and concise.

"We're always interested in good marketing and promotional ideas and encourage you to bring them from both your company and other retailers.

"We appreciate product training and will attempt to make our salespeople available as often as you can offer it.

"If you will offer me your best pricing, terms, and advertising co-op without haggling, we'll be able to focus our time on increasing sales.

"Please tell me about all your specials, promotions, close-outs, scratch & dents ....

"I'll consider products you would like us to try if you'll assist me with returns or moving them sideways if they don't sell.

"I'll work with you on the buy-ins and re-ups your company imposes if you'll help me find ways to make them fit our business."

Being professional and business-like doesn't require being disrespectful.

142

A savvy rep has a bag full of tricks.

Many of the devices for inducing retailers to buy are straightforward economic incentives: quantity discounts, introductory pricing, cumulative discounts, year-end rebates, throw-ins, limited-time specials, return options, advertising co-op, free freight, extended terms ....

Others are requirements to demonstrate commitment to the product: opening orders, stocking requirements, buy-ins, periodic re-ups ....

Occasionally there are overt appeals to personal interests: trips and prizes for owners and buyers, spiffs to salesmen, etc. (all direct conflicts of interest for the store).

Then there are comparisons to sales of other dealers and markets as well as to previous years. Often they include implicit or explicit threats to broaden distribution.

None of these are inherently unfair—indeed a manufacturer must promote sales of his products and ensure that his dealers represent them appropriately. Conflicts arise when aggressive manufacturers and reps press quantities or products that the retailer is unlikely to resell easily or at a reasonable profit.

143

An experienced buyer is a worthy opponent.

Smart retailers are hardly defenseless. They've seen most of a rep's tactics and have developed responses and techniques for coping with them.

Pitches to try unattractive products evoke friendly procrastination (since outright rejection is confrontational and counterproductive). Continued pressure might bring the retailer's suggestion of taking the products on consignment or with a return option.

Quantity discount requirements are sometimes met by scheduling split or delayed shipments. (Retailers with sufficient clout dispense with quantity discounts by negotiating end-column pricing on every purchase regardless of timing.)

A rep's frustration over low sales is soothed by an offer to gather the store's salespeople so the rep can better train them on the products.

Implied threats to broaden distribution prompt similarly implied threats to reduce orders and/or take on competitive products.

And everything is conveyed with politeness to avoid hard feelings that might lead the rep to do something out of spite.

Many retailers tell stories of "taking the rep outside and showing him whose name is over the door."

The story seldom concludes with the rep saying, "Oh, yes, thank you; I forgot. Let me be more reasonable." The more likely result is increased confrontation or pent-up aggression. The rep will find a way to repay the insolence.

Animosity seldom serves a useful purpose.

A high opening order calls for scheduled shipping and order revisions.

Opening order requirements are meant to demonstrate that the dealer intends to stock an agreeable representation of the products. Fair enough. But the concept goes wrong when the requirements include excessive quantities and products with little resale potential.

Some dealers negotiate opening orders into split shipments so they can "make room on the sales floor." The better products sell through, leaving room for the balance of their quantities. Orders for the remaining shipments can be revised, substituting better sellers for the weak sellers. As long as the total order isn't reduced significantly, the rep seldom complains.

145

This year's purchases are next year's baseline.

Manufacturers like and expect their sales with a dealer to increase from year to year. Most sales managers provide their reps with annual comparison reports. When a report shows a decline, the dealer should expect scrutiny, often pressure, and sometimes threats.

As a result many dealers plan their purchases carefully, allocating them to align with the manufacturer's fiscal years. Some even shift orders to alternative manufacturers to keep sales trends with important manufacturers smooth.

When aberrations are unavoidable, for example as a result of a large one-time customer order, some dealers notify the rep and manufacturer (in writing) of the reasons for the spike, so they can later remind them of reasonable expectations.

When we recently placed our annual spring order with one of our largest manufacturers, we were surprised that the national sales manager called to thank us. A few weeks later when we won an award for the largest dealer increase, we knew we were in trouble.

We discovered their fiscal year ends February 28th. We submitted our order February 25th, a week or two earlier than in previous years. It nearly doubled our volume with them for their fiscal year, making us heroes.

In their next fiscal year, not only can we not match that new doubled level, our purchases will be almost nothing. We'll be their most disappointing dealer. That will, no doubt, create much anxiety for both of us.

Displays are a rep's judgment of product commitment.

Regardless of how much we promote a product, how often our salesmen show it, and how many we sell, a rep's impression of our store's efforts for his products will be formed largely by our displays. Whether the displays have any real impact on sales is irrelevant. Additionally, the rep is unlikely to be satisfied until his products get at least what he considers fair display emphasis relative to his competitors' products.

Before every rep visit (which should always be scheduled), it's good practice to confirm that his products are adequately represented in displays, in good condition, priced correctly and competitively, and promotional materials are used properly. (Yes, these things should always be in order—but when is retail perfect?)

147

Careful what you dish out as one day you might have to eat it.

When a line doesn't sell well or we find another product we'd rather sell, we stop ordering. When the rep asks us why, we seldom reveal our intentions or willingly give up the line.

Sometimes it's because we think we might someday order again. More often it's because we don't like the idea of a competitor getting the line.

If a manufacturer and rep have been honest and straightforward in their dealings with us, it's only fair to amicably end the relationship and allow them to make their livings.

Word gets around quickly if we don't deal fairly. And at some time in the future this rep or this manufacturer might have a product or line we'd like.

148

"Restraint of trade" is simple but serious semantics.

It's commonly understood and expected that retailers stock only products that are profitable; we can't work for free. It's also understood that products become less profitable as their distribution broadens. So it follows that as a supplier adds more dealers to a market some retailers will reduce or eliminate their representation of the products. All this is standard and legitimate business practice.

But the phrasing we use in discussing this with our supplier is serious legal business. We can say we handle their products because we make reasonable margins with them (due to few competitors), or that we won't handle their products because we can't make sufficient margins with them (due to too many competitors). But it's illegal to agree with a supplier—in writing, verbally, or by any other method—to sell their products only if they don't sell them to a competitor.

The difference may seem trivial but legally it's critical. The implications of an FTC investigation or complaint are huge—just complying with a subpoena and hiring a defense lawyer is enough to sink many companies. Whether the inquiry is justified and whether we can make a strong argument against it make little difference if we can't afford the defense. (Yes, this is not the way our justice system is supposed to work but unfortunately it's the current reality.) And even if we win, our expenses aren't recoverable.

It goes without saying that written correspondence (including email) should carefully avoid any suggestion, proposal, agreement, or threat that might be considered an attempt to restrict competition. (Some say any discussion at all of a competitor with a supplier is assuming dangerous risks.)

In 1996 Toys R Us was charged by the FTC with restraint of trade for pressuring its suppliers not to sell their products to the warehouse clubs. The FTC didn't question Toys R Us' right to refuse to purchase from the manufacturers, but took issue with their forcing manufacturers into agreements not to sell the products to competitors.

The case took four years and consumed millions of dollars as well as countless executive hours. The court's ultimate decision—that Toys R Us did illegally restrain trade—was an expensive loss for Toy R Us requiring huge ongoing compliance expenses and ultimately fines. But even if they had won, the case still would have been catastrophic.

149

Reps are the industry's grapevine.

Retailers often tell their reps about their effective promotions, potential sales, recent successes, and future plans—occasionally even their challenges, failures, and frustrations. (Many reps say psychological counseling is part of their job descriptions.) Reps also know how dealers are reordering and paying their bills. As a result vendor reps can be a rich source of information, especially concerning competitors.

Good reps are careful about what they pass on, but many others don't resist the temptation.

We should remember that our reps often go directly from our stores to our competitors', and what we tell them would make fascinating topics of conversation at their next stops.

A good rule of thumb is to tell our reps only what we want to tell our competitors. (Many are reliable conduits for messages and misinformation we'd like to convey.)

150

Your rep can make your sales ideas standard industry practice.

One of the more valuable services a rep can provide is sharing the innovative marketing ideas and methods he sees in his other dealers' stores. They can increase our sales and his.

Most retailers are only too happy to brag about their marketing successes. They realize their reps will share them with other retailers, but most of those retailers aren't direct competitors. What they don't realize is how quickly a good idea spreads through this network and comes back home.

It's heady stuff to have our innovations adopted widely, but we need to consider whether we want to help our competitors discover and adopt them so quickly.

In the 1980s we began offering a "Guaranteed Trade Back" with all piano purchases—customers who buy a piano from us get a certificate that says they can trade it back at any time for the full amount paid. It's an attractive assurance for first-time buyers and also appeals to those who think they might eventually move up to a better piano.

Word spread, primarily through the rep network, and within a few years such guarantees became standard practice with piano retailers across the country—including all of our local competitors. Now when we talk up our Guaranteed Trade Back many customers are unimpressed because, as they say, "Everybody does that." (Adding that we originated the GTB is interesting trivia but with little influence on sales.)

We also came up with the idea of hosting meetings and parties for local interior designers' associations in an effort to establish relationships and encourage including grand pianos in their designs. We invited our Steinway rep to speak at one of those meetings; he liked the idea so much that Steinway soon published it as part of its recommended promotions series.

Not to be outdone, Yamaha quickly adopted the idea and trained its dealers in precisely our plan. (A few years later our Steinway rep asked if we had ever tried *their* interior designer promotion.)

It was about this time we realized that our older retailer friends listen well and talk little.

Employment brokerage is sometimes a rep service too.

Reps can be a valuable resource in recruiting employees, but a dangerous nuisance in keeping them. They know who's selling and where to reach them, and some can be surprisingly accommodating with the information. They become particularly dangerous (or, depending on your perspective, helpful) after they've changed manufacturers or severed relationships with a retailer.

(Perhaps the best use of their recruiting talents is in recommending our competitors' best people as proven salesmen who "deserve better opportunities.")

I once asked all of our piano manufacturer reps for help in finding good salespeople.

All were eager to be of service. The better reps offered the names of competitive dealers' salespeople. Some others added previous dealers' employees.

One, however, dictated a list of his current dealers' best salespeople. (To his dubious credit, he asked me not to mention where I had gotten the names.)

152

Be kind to the rep
—you'll see him again.

Recycling of reps is a common practice in most industries. Manufacturers love to hire salesmen who have experience, know the territory, and already have contacts. (In many cases those criteria are apparently more important than their work habits, effectiveness, or reputations.)

As a result, it's good policy to treat all reps courteously regardless of how we feel about them, the product they offer, or how they've treated us. Chances are good they'll be back at some point, possibly with products we'd like to represent.

COMPETITORS

153

We always have competitors;
our customers see to it.

Customers need another store to compare us to. "Shop around and compare," is the most ubiquitous of consumer advice. Shopping ensures a more informed choice, uncovers price differences, and sometimes creates negotiating leverage.

If we don't have local competitors, our customers look out-of-town or on the Internet. Not having competitors isn't the boon we sometimes imagine since shoppers simply assume (often correctly) our prices are high, resent our "monopoly," and are discouraged from buying regardless of our pricing and service.

Sometimes customers' searches attract new competitors. When they call similar stores asking for our products, they're encouraging those stores to stock them. (One customer can make a lot of calls.) Some customers directly entice competitors to add our products and services or move into our market, pointing out the local shortage of supply.

A small-town competitor in band instrument rentals had a policy of buying a budgeted number of rental instruments per year. When those were rented, he simply turned customers away.

Those customers were forced to call out-of-town stores and it didn't take many of those calls to get our attention. Our salesman went directly to the schools and offered to host a group meeting with guaranteed instrument availability. The band directors quickly agreed, happy to resolve what they considered a recurring shortage.

As a result of those customers' calls, the local retailer lost almost all the profitable rental business in his own town.

A weak competitor is a useful nuisance.

The best retail scenario is to have competitors who are several steps behind us—disorganized, under-financed, technologically challenged, less desirable products, poorly trained staff …. Such stores provide the comparison our customers need and allow us to stand out in contrast.

They also deter new competitors from entering the market. Retailing, like physics, abhors a vacuum. When there are too few stores, locals are encouraged to enter the business, out-of-town stores spot an easy opportunity, and manufacturers lure dealers to town. A few struggling competitors make the opportunity appear not so easy.

Having no competitors isn't nirvana—having weak competitors is.

When you think you're on top, you don't do much climbing.

It's easy to get lazy when our competitors are far behind us—we're getting most of the business anyway so there's little incentive to improve.

But fat and happy is a precarious position in retailing, and always temporary. Bad habits and inefficiencies become entrenched and we fall behind market standards and expectations, becoming easy targets for more progressive retailers.

An energetic competitor is often the push we need to keep improving.

> "Business success contains the seeds of its own destruction. The more successful you are, the more people want a chunk of your business and then another chunk and then another until there is nothing left. I believe that the prime responsibility of a manager is to guard constantly against other people's attacks and to inculcate this guardian attitude in the people under his or her management."
>
> —Andy Grove

156

A good competitor creates traffic for everyone.

Competitors' advertising and promotion make us nervous—we resent the business they get from it, thinking it could or should be ours. We overlook the fact that our competitors' efforts might also be increasing our business.

Helpful competitor advertising is focused on market creation, not market harvesting. Ads that emphasize low price bring few new people into the market; they're designed to cash out customers already shopping. While they sometimes create a temporary surge of traffic, they're likely to take more existing prospects than they create new ones.

Ads and promotion meant to attract new customers can benefit all the stores in a market. The effects of such ads are seldom as immediate as harvest ads, so it's difficult to fully appreciate their value, but over the long run their effect can be significant for everyone.

Piano rental is an attractive and profitable business. Pianos often stay out on rent for years, depreciate little, and rental income is as dependable as an annuity.

In the late '90s both of our local piano rental competitors reached retirement age and, at virtually the same time, offered to sell us their businesses. Calculating a value for their existing rentals was simple enough, but estimating how much of their future business we'd get was more challenging.

As it turned out the total number of rentals in the market after we purchased their companies was about 25 percent less than before. We speculate that many potential customers don't consider renting a piano until someone plants the seed. Our competitors' advertising, the visibility of their locations, and their activity in the community were creating awareness that we couldn't easily replace.

Good isn't good enough; only best gets the sale.

Second-best among competitors isn't a consolation, it's a catastrophe. Our customers never choose the second-best value for their money; they choose the best (in their eyes) every time. No matter how close the contest, when we're deemed second-best we get nothing.

Customers evaluate many criteria in each sale—product quality, price, store convenience, location, sales help, hours, displays .... And each customer weighs each factor slightly differently (creating an opportunity for perceptive retailers to exploit the niches). But ultimately only the store the customer judges best overall gets the sale.

Coach Lombardi had it right, "Winning isn't everything, it's the only thing."

> When you stop trying to be better, you stop being good.

158

To be better we have to know compared to what.

A smart coach adjusts his team's strategies to combat the strengths and strategies of opposing teams. If he couldn't see his opponents, he wouldn't know what to change. He might win the easy games, but against worthy opponents he'd be beaten without knowing how or why.

A retailer, too, needs to know what his competitors are doing—what products they offer, how they price them, how they present them, what terms they offer .... Only then can he see where he's winning and losing and what he needs to improve to win.

We get some of that information through customer feedback and lost sales—but that's the slow and expensive way. Much more efficient is seeing it for ourselves.

Sometimes we can visit anonymously. Or we can make our visit a friendly hello; extending an invitation or sharing some industry news provides a good reason.

If we wouldn't be welcome, we have to send someone. Their descriptions aren't as good as firsthand experience but several combined can create an accurate picture.

> "You can't expect to win unless you know why you lose."
>
> — Benjamin Lipson

Salespeople give competitors more credit than they deserve.

Our salespeople often overestimate our competitors. They tend to assume our competitors' stores are bigger, their selections broader, their products more appealing, their salespeople more knowledgeable, their service more reliable, and their prices lower than they actually are. Such insecurity can sap confidence that otherwise would reassure and encourage shoppers to buy from us.

Our competitors face the same challenges and cope with the same problems we do. They have good and bad days, experienced and inexperienced salesmen, good and poor selections, up and down employees, and fresh and stale inventory. They occasionally have insufficient expertise, people out sick, products out of stock, suppliers that can't ship, systems that fail, too many customers or phone calls at once, etc.

Neither they nor we are perfect, but there are always differences. Before we can convey to our customers the benefits and advantages of our store and offerings, we must understand and appreciate them ourselves.

> As part of sales training we require new salespeople to visit our competitors and provide a report on their stores, salespeople, products, and presentations. The fresh perspective of a new salesperson resembles that of a shopper, and his assessment of their strengths and weaknesses gives him an understanding of what he needs to do to succeed.
>
> At the next sales meeting his report is shared and discussed with the veteran salespeople.

160

We don't see our competitors' happy customers.

The complaints we hear about our competitors aren't a balanced picture. Only their dissatisfied customers come see us; their satisfied customers have bought, are happy, and have no reason to be in our stores.

Whether the result of mistakes, misunderstandings, or unrealistic expectations, even a great store has a few unhappy customers. Although sometimes vocal, they're often not representative of typical business experiences.

Remember, while we're seeing their mistakes they're seeing ours. Agitating and aggravating are likely to be repaid in kind.

Little bits of knowledge shape potent strategies.

News articles, public records, hiring interviews with previous employees, conversations with manufacturers' reps, service providers, and customers—information about competitors comes from many sources. It provides details about their sales, financial health, niches, and marketing strategies, as well as their challenges and vulnerabilities.

Among the things we're likely to discover are tactics they're using against us, brands we'd like to have, employees we'd like to hire, customers and key influencers that warrant pursuing, product opportunities we've overlooked, effective marketing concepts, improved operating methods, useful suppliers, expansion plans, and future directions.

We can't accumulate all this information at once, and we're unlikely to remember the details when we need them, so it makes sense to maintain a file on each competitor, present and potential. Whenever we come across information, we can cut it out or write it down and drop it in the file. When an opportunity arises, the accumulated information might provide just the background we need to make a strategic decision and act on it.

My brother occasionally sends letters to our competitors reminding them of our interest in buying their companies—especially when he hears they're facing cash-flow challenges, have hit bumps, are burning out, or are reaching retirement age. A few respond, others put the letter in their files, and most keep the information in the back of their minds. Four times in the last decade those contacts led to profitable acquisitions of assets, good people, and on-going business.

Other companies would surely have been interested in these acquisitions—and some would have become new and formidable competitors in our market. Fortunately they didn't make the contact and get the information at the critical times.

The measure of a competitor is the price he can get.

Our low-price competitor probably isn't as crazy as he seems. He knows what price he has to offer to get the sale.

If his product is inferior, his reputation poorer, or the confidence he evokes lacking, he must sell for less than we do. His price reflects differences he has to make up for.

If his pricing isn't sufficient to pay expenses and keep the store operating, he'll discover and deal with that later. For now he's doing what he has to do to make a sale and keep cash flowing.

Value, not price, makes sales.

Despite what a few customers would have us believe, they're not looking for just any product that qualifies for its name. They have a specific need to fill and they know the choice they make will determine how well that need is met.

Selling exactly the same products in exactly the same way and on the same terms as our competitor is not a promising formula for profitability. Creating and emphasizing differences is a more lucrative strategy than being drawn into a price war.

But to do this salespeople must recognize and appreciate the differences. They must know the products—their own and their competitors'—and be prepared to show and explain how they differ. Accumulating such knowledge takes time and effort—and consequently new and uneducated salespeople compete on price.

When we show shoppers more value they'll give us a better price.

> "There is scarcely anything in the world that some man cannot make a little worse and sell a little cheaper. The person who buys on price alone is this man's lawful prey."
>
> —John Ruskin

164

Good service is the delusion of bad stores.

Many retailers claim the difference between their stores and their competitors' is customer service. The irony is apparently lost on them that their competitors say and believe the same thing.

Even superstores with notoriously bad service cite customer service as a competitive advantage. Meanwhile, customers have trouble naming any store with good service—but can name plenty with bad service.

"Good customer service" rarely really is. Guiding a customer to products because they're not logically arranged and marked, showing products to a customer because they aren't out or displayed adequately, and looking up prices because they aren't tagged are not good service; they're bad retailing.

A store that claims "good service" as its primary differentiation almost always has anemic or negative profits.

"Everybody says they provide great service these days, and except for Nordstrom and Ritz-Carlton and a few others, they're all full of shit."

—Sol Price, Price Clubs

165

The last 20% of market share isn't worth having.

Unless we're a government-sanctioned monopoly we can't get 100 percent market share—and we shouldn't want it.

Consider the relentless price shopper who buys only when he finds a deal that defies its expenses. Liquidations, distress sales, bankruptcies, and tax sales are his scavenging grounds. Let our competitors do those.

Other customers take pride in being different. They get their thrills finding obscure offerings from small, often quirky, vendors. Obscurity isn't a promising marketing plan.

One hundred percent is a nice goal for salespeople, but management needs practical and realistic plans and strategies for employing the store's resources.

166

An aggressive competitor deserves the bad deals.

"If we don't take the deal our competitor will" is strange logic for taking a loss. We should help him get it; it will keep him busy while we pursue profitable sales.

It seems perverse to a salesperson to let a sale get away, especially after working hard to win it. But some sales don't make sense: the price wouldn't cover expenses, the customer wouldn't be happy, anticipated service and problems are too high, collection is unlikely ....

Let them go. Sometimes when we raise the level of what we'll accept, our competitor does, too—eventually. (Competitors are never as smart as we are, but occasionally they're not as dumb as they appear.)

> When we rent musical instruments we require a credit check. In the past if a customer didn't pass, couldn't make a deposit, and couldn't be interested in buying, we always considered it a customer service to refer him to our competitor who didn't check credit—until he went out of business.

167

A niche is a backdoor left open for new competitors.

If we don't meet market demand for a product, its potential buyers will find someone who will. That seemingly insignificant niche, if profitable, might prove to be the sliver of soil on the side of the cliff that allows a great oak to take root.

The niche can be products or services we don't offer, or it might be specialized knowledge and expertise, demographics we've ignored, relationships we haven't cultivated, terms we haven't offered, even an image in contrast to our own.

But it's always an opportunity for someone with energy and focus. And often our competitors show us that the niches are much bigger than we ever suspected.

Guitar Center's flagship store in Hollywood is a huge cavern, stocked to its high ceilings with virtually every brand musicians dream about. You would think it suicidal to open a small shop in its shadow.

And yet a half dozen or so small guitar shops have set up nearby. Each has found a niche — left-hand guitars, vintage instruments, custom finishes and hardware, bass guitars, rentals, trades, consignment, repair service, etc.

The former CEO of this two-billion dollar chain told me niche players were the threat he feared most. He believed that they would gradually surround his stores, picking off little chunks of the market until what remained no longer supported his company.

168

Every market makes room for hustle and determination.

There's always a place for a determined retailer with common sense and a willingness to work. He might, at times, be swimming upstream, but that doesn't mean he can't make it.

Many independent retailers have despaired when faced with superstores taking chunks of their market share; meanwhile those determined to stay and willing to adapt have learned to coexist and thrive.

Huge chains enjoy advantages of large outside investment: giant selections and displays, expensive data management systems, powerful purchasing leverage, etc. But local independents have potential advantages too, including on-site expertise and decision making, attention to detail, personal and community relationships, and long-term dedicated management.

Small retailers can also react quickly to opportunities and market changes. While big stores are bound by entrenched systems and operating methods, large scale purchasing agreements, and layers of management, small stores can accumulate information, make decisions, re-channel resources, and begin implementation all in the same day.

169

An unprofitable competitor dies for years.

The problems of an unprofitable store compound and become hard to hide. Inventories shrink, manufacturers search for alternative representation, employees become disgruntled and quit, customers become frustrated and move their business, creditors take legal action, and rumors and speculations spread irrepressibly.

We're sure the end is near—the bank will foreclose, key manufacturers will jump ship, a creditor will force liquidation, they'll miss payrolls and lose their employees, the tax man will padlock the door, or they'll simply throw in the towel.

Yet ownership is oblivious to what seems obvious to everyone else; indeed they would be offended at the suggestion that the store might go out of business. They defy the seemingly inevitable and hang on—for years. Partial payments keep creditors at bay, hungry new vendors front more merchandise, cash is extracted from real estate or personal assets, a relative or an over-eager bank extends a loan ....

None of which fixes the underlying problem—the store continues to lose money. They're weak and getting weaker, but don't expect a funeral any time soon.

170

Losing a competitor isn't always cause for celebration.

It's tempting to wish our competitors away—they are, by definition, nuisances. But despite the frustrations they cause us, we're often better off with them than without them.

By the time a weak competitor is ready to close he's usually having minimal effect on us and is providing the favorable comparisons we need.

When one competitor leaves, another typically takes his place. The new competitor often understands even less about his costs, and his learning curve is expensive—for both him and us.

The competitor we know is often preferable to the competitor we don't.

171

A retailer's effectiveness can be measured by the animosity of his competitors.

Being liked by our competitors is not something to be proud of. If they don't feel constant pressure from our products and offerings, we're not doing our job.

Good sportsmanship doesn't exist in retailing—only complaints, excuses, and accusations: "They give their products away," "Their salespeople lie and promise things they don't deliver," "Their product is cheaper because it's inferior."

The stakes in retailing are high. When we beat a competitor regularly, it's not respect we garner but fear and resentment.

Once, at an industry convention, a friend made a derogatory remark about a competitor who had just thanked him for their cordial relationship. Knowing nothing of their history and looking for a little excitement in discord, I said, "He seems nice enough to me. What's the problem?"

"He's a smart-ass. He knows he lost two big sales to us last week. That cordial bit was just his way of saying 'You might think you're good, but you really don't bother me at all.'"

It would have been interesting to explore the topic further, but my friend's face had gotten red and his humor was turning unpleasant. This was obviously a hot button.

Despite my friend's bluster, I always suspected his competitor was getting the better of him. While I doubted the competitor's sincerity, my friend couldn't contain his hostility.

172

A company is known by the people it keeps.

Lots of components make up a retail store: a building, inventory, products, policies, systems, décor, organization, marketing, and a thousand more details. But none of these is as important or as defining as its people.

A great store can only be built with great people. Their quality is visible in every aspect of the store's facilities, methods, and operation—indeed the store is the product of the people.

No other element is as critical and no other element can make up for a store's people.

173

It's not 10-20% more;
good people produce 200-300% more.

A dedicated employee doesn't just get his work done—he finds ways to do it faster and better. A disinterested employee doesn't just do a little less—he often doesn't get started.

This is true for all employees, but it's most noticeable with salespeople because their sales are easily and commonly tracked. The best salespeople often sell two to three times the average, and even higher multiples of the low producers.

Even after significantly higher pay, better employees are virtually always more profitable.

> "Half effort does not produce half results. It produces no results."
>
> **—Hamilton Holt**

174

The most valuable talent in retail is recognizing talent in others.

Good hires attract customers, create sales, make prudent decisions, seize opportunities, reduce mistakes, provide good example, inspire co-workers, and contribute to a positive culture.

Poor hires repel customers, deter sales, squander opportunities, increase mistakes, lower standards, and drag down morale. They are among the most expensive mistakes a company makes.

The cliché "Our people are our most important asset," is inspiring and politically wise, but it really should be "Our good people are our most important asset."

But identifying a potential hire as good or poor is one of retail's greatest arts and challenges. What will be obvious, sometimes painfully, after several weeks or months of work is barely perceptible from an application, résumé, and interview. (It was likely a retailer who observed that the closest a person comes to perfection is on a résumé and job application.)

We once calculated unscientifically that a third of our hires were mistakes, and a third were tolerable. Only with the final third did we get what we had hoped for.

The third that were mistakes had serious and intolerable flaws—dishonesty, irresponsibility, inability to get along with co-workers, etc. They were eventually replaced, although usually more slowly than they should have been and always at considerable expense. Not only were time, effort, and payroll wasted but significant customer opportunities were squandered.

The tolerable third tried to meet expectations but lacked some essential trait or ability—most often drive or focus. Replacing them would have been more profitable, but usually we've lived with them—changing employees is expensive and disruptive as well as unpleasant.

The third correctly chosen were highly profitable investments. They became successful and valued team members and created followings of happy customers.

Realization of this ratio and its economics inspired us to focus on and refine our hiring skills.

Hire slowly, fire quickly.

We get this backward, don't we?

When a job is open, we're eager to get a person onboard and get the work going again. We tend to assume applicants have the same values we do, and because we have little experience with the various problems that afflict many of them, we're unsuspecting and miss the clues.

Once we've hired them and invested time and effort in training them, we hesitate to fix our mistakes. We try to salvage employees with coaching and more training, even though we've learned it's almost always futile.

We'd do better to reverse this tendency—choose our hires slowly and carefully, and replace them immediately when our mistakes become apparent.

176

Good hiring tests time management; bad hiring destroys it.

The hiring process is time-intensive, especially when done correctly. Taking applications, interviewing, checking background and references, and other minor but critical tasks of hiring don't fit easily into a retailer's schedule. But there are some opportunities to conserve time without compromising results.

An employee can filter inquiry calls quickly with a few questions. If the caller doesn't meet the basic requirements or his work experience is a total mismatch, a polite explanation of what is sought can wrap up the call.

Other applicants will eliminate themselves if asked if they can pass a background check, drug test, and credit check (even if we don't do them all).

The job application should include some open-ended, essay-style questions to quickly sort out those without the necessary communication skills.

For the remaining candidates, credit checks and preliminary background checks are quick and inexpensive and can be run by a staff member.

Then previous employers can be called. Although many employers are reluctant to provide much real insight, it's rarely a complete shutout and even a little information from those who know the applicant's work habits can be invaluable.

Interviewing is the most time-consuming step, so it's saved for last when the applicant stack is culled to a few. A lower manager can do initial interviews, selecting only the top few candidates for top management's consideration.

When the process is thorough and careful, we need it less often.

The applicant pool is not a cross section of the population.

The group of people in the job market at any time is not at all a representative sample of the general population. It's skewed to the lowest quality of the workforce and heavily weighted with undesirables and unemployables.

Many candidates have obvious flaws such as poor appearance or communication skills. They stay in the pool long term and apply for many jobs.

Some of the rest look good but have underlying flaws (poor work habits, psychological imbalances, drug or alcohol dependencies, criminal histories, etc.). Careful companies don't choose them, so these applicants tend to stay in the pool for some time. They're occasionally hired by companies that don't do their homework but they're typically back in the pool many times.

Of those without the above flaws, some would qualify as adequate but are lacking in the focus and drive of a good employee. They would show up and do the required work, but contribute little of what makes a company outstanding.

A few really good candidates go through the pool but they're usually hired quickly—sometimes by companies that are just lucky, but most often by companies that have great hiring processes, do extensive homework, and choose carefully. These candidates aren't in the pool long and typically don't come back to it at all.

> One of our department managers with long-term hiring experience estimates that less than one in twenty applicants is a suitable candidate for a job and one in a hundred is an outstanding choice.

178

The best candidates aren't applicants.

Few outstanding workers are ever without a job. When they change jobs, it's typically because they're lured to better opportunities by astute employers who recognize their abilities.

Even in downsizings, companies rarely let their stars get away—they find them other jobs within the company. And when a business closes, its best people have typically impressed enough customers, competitors, and friends that other opportunities are waiting for them.

Consequently not many outstanding candidates answer employment ads and go through the normal application process. In most cases they have to be sought and enticed, through friends and acquaintances, in other jobs, and by soliciting recommendations.

179

When applying is difficult only the desperate apply.

An extensive and inconvenient application process discourages the most desirable candidates—those who already have jobs but might consider another opportunity. The candidates most willing to navigate a complex process are those who have lost their jobs, often with good reason, and are in dire need of another; they have ready résumés and plenty of time for long applications and appointments.

Requirements such as applying by mail and submitting a résumé make the applicant stack more manageable but are likely to cull the rare gem we're looking for. To attract that prize we have to make inquiring and applying easy.

In advertising we can include an attractive job description, specify the pay, and encourage inquiries by phone or email. Yes, this means lots of inquiries to deal with. But an employee can sort through them with a few quick questions, getting more information from the better ones, and encouraging the best to come talk.

180

Hiring experience is a quick fix; hiring motivation is the long-term fix.

An experienced candidate gets up to speed quickly and gets the work going again. He's a fast solution to a pressing problem.

But if the experienced candidate lacks motivation and dedication, his short-term advantages are soon offset by long-term underperformance.

A motivated employee will learn what he needs to know to do his job. Experience is a head start, but motivation soon catches up and overtakes it.

The ideal, of course, is a motivated, experienced candidate. Unfortunately they're both rare and expensive—but often worth the search and the money.

181

Education is a poor predictor of retail results.

Education teaches critical thinking and is generally indicative of persistence. The field studied is not as important as the acquired ability to learn and adapt. It is a tool that can be useful in any type of work.

Nevertheless, many retailers say education is an unreliable indicator of success in retailing, and consequently it ranks down their list of desirable criteria. Perhaps the reasons are that studying by itself doesn't get things done, or that social skills aren't part of degree requirements. Some might even say that many degree-holders are educated beyond their common sense. (Who doesn't know a Ph.D. who seems lost to humanity?)

Education can indeed be a useful tool in retailing, but only when its owner is able and willing to put it to work.

182

No skill or ability makes up for lack of integrity.

A candidate who doesn't have integrity is unemployable. Skills, abilities, knowledge, experience, and intelligence only make him more dangerous as they are soon turned against us.

People with criminal records are particularly risky. We're sometimes tempted to believe that a person who once made a mistake has learned a lesson and won't repeat the error—indeed many candidates who've been in trouble are amazingly convincing. And it's natural to want to help a person who's trying to help himself.

But few people are caught the first time they commit a crime. Most work their way up from petty to more serious crimes, and are caught and convicted only after crime has become a way of life.

Background checks and previous job references aren't just smart hiring, they're indispensable in protecting our customers, our companies, our employees, and ourselves.

> When in doubt about whether a person's background should disqualify him from consideration, imagine yourself a defendant in a lawsuit concerning a crime this employee committed against a customer or employee. The plaintiff's attorney aims to prove that you should have recognized this employee would be a risk. Could he convince the jury?

Experience isn't always a plus.

An experienced employee can occasionally be a good hire, especially if he's a proven performer or has important customer relationships that will come with him.

But experience also brings bad habits, and sometimes retraining is more difficult and expensive than starting over.

Often when a competitor's employee applies with us it's because he's performing poorly and under pressure to improve. If we take him, we only relieve the competitor of his problem and assume it ourselves. If the competitor hires smarter next time, he's moved forward while we've moved back.

True, such a potential employee sometimes has useful competitive information. But most of it is usually available in an interview.

184

Relatives are easy to hire, hard to fire.

Our employees find out about job openings early (sometimes before we do), and husbands, wives, or children looking for a job often get a quick call. The applicant needs a job and we need an employee. Since they're related to someone already on staff, we assume their work will be similar. It's a quick and simple solution.

But the outcome is often anything but simple. When one of them is unhappy with management or the company, the stakes are doubled. Employee quarrels are ratcheted up as one defends the other. Family spats and divorces are played out at work. Vacations, family emergencies, and health challenges take both away at once. It's almost impossible to address the underperformance of one without alienating the other. And firing one means losing two.

Better applicants are almost always available, not as quickly but without the risks and complications.

185

Only dumb businesses need discrimination laws.

Discrimination laws are superfluous to well-run businesses. High-quality candidates are too rare and valuable for a business to choose by any criteria except performance potential.

Retail is a high-stakes competition and the winner is almost always the store that assembles the best combination of people. Like a championship sports team, a great company is often an odd collection of motley characters with only one thing in common: excellent skills in their respective jobs.

Imposing any other hiring criteria—race, age, sex, nationality, beliefs, sexual orientation, or anything else—only compromises a store's ability to compete.

186

A job interview is an oral exam conducted as casual conversation.

An interview has a precise purpose. In a relatively short conversation we want to get an accurate read of the candidate's personality, talents, habits, motivation, attitudes, values, work ethic, knowledge, goals, plans, etc. We collect specific information about how they communicate, how driven they are for results, which aspects of the job would appeal to them and which would give them trouble, and how long they're likely to stay.

Despite this focus, the style most likely to draw out the information is casual conversation—a relaxed candidate speaks more openly and allows his true personality and attitudes to come through.

Good interviewers begin by breaking the ice, usually with small talk about background or common experiences. Only after the candidate has relaxed does the interviewer move on to his list of probing questions.

187

All applicants are smart until they speak.

We sometimes "fall in love" with candidates we interview, especially if they're friendly, make a nice appearance, or have useful experience.

First impressions are important in retail but they're only part of the story. All applicants have strengths and faults, advantages and detriments, and our job in an interview is to uncover them.

Our best tools are subjective, open-ended questions that require the candidate to expose his attitudes and philosophies. We should ask the questions as casually as possible, then let him do the talking—don't help him with the answers.

When we find something that merits pursuing, we should ask for elaboration: "That's interesting. Tell me more."

Here are some of the interview questions we've found useful:

- Tell me about some things you've done that you're proud of.
- What do you feel are your greatest strengths? Weaknesses?
- Describe a normal workday at your last job.
- What did you like best? What did you like least?
- What will your manager say about your work?
- What do you consider your most noteworthy accomplishments on that job?
- What was your most frustrating experience?
- What was your most satisfying experience?
- What are some things the company might have done to be more successful?
- What did you do to make yourself more effective in your work?
- Describe the ideal job for you.
- What motivates you to put forth your greatest effort?
- What are your other job possibilities and how do you feel about them?
- Where do you see yourself in three years?
- What goals do you have for your career?
- What will it take to attain those goals?
- What steps have you taken toward attaining them?
- Why do you want this job?
- What do you think differentiates you from the other applicants?
- What do you know about this company?
- What else can you tell me that would help me make this decision?

188

Their questions reveal more than their answers.

Perhaps the most telling interview question is, "What questions do you have for me?" Their response is a strong indicator of their motivation and values.

The best responses show interest in the job, the company, training, and future opportunities. Poor responses concern time off, vacation, benefits, drug and background checks, etc.

Not having questions usually indicates little thought given to the job or a desire to find almost any job. (The exception is when the applicant says he's already talked at length to an employee who gave detailed answers to all his questions—an excellent answer and strong indication of both understanding and interest.)

189

Con men do great interviews; conscientious applicants often do poorly.

Job interviewees should be nervous. They recognize the interview as a test that determines their future. They're in strange territory, talking to an unfamiliar authority figure with decision power over their career. They often fear an inhospitable grilling and have agonized over the questions. The more they want the job, the more nervous they should be.

Perhaps candidates who aren't nervous should be a bigger concern than those who are. Among those without normal fears are those who don't care about the job, practiced liars, and hardened criminals.

The best indicator of future performance is past performance.

Lots of candidates talk a good game, but talk and performance are often inversely related. Experience has taught many what should be done, but that doesn't mean they have the drive and motivation to do it. Even trying a potential employee out doesn't guarantee long-term performance, as anyone can push oneself to uncharacteristic performance for short periods.

The most reliable indicator of how a candidate will perform is how he has performed previously. If he was focused and driven in his last job he will almost surely be the same in the next. Jobs change but personalities don't.

(Past performance is less reliable when two jobs call for opposite personality traits. While a great accountant might make a good engineer, he probably wouldn't be a great salesman. And the world has yet to see a good salesman who could be a good accountant.)

191

A candidate who manages his own business poorly will manage ours worse.

A credit report is an excellent predictor of a candidate's organizational skills and reliability. It reflects personal habits that inevitably carry over to work. In addition, financial pressure is a distraction at minimum, increased temptation to dishonesty at worst.

(Running a credit report is legal in many areas if the job involves handling money and the candidate consents. The job application can include the consent.)

Occasionally an unavoidable event (e.g., a serious medical problem, divorce) creates a temporary and unrepresentative credit record. We can sometimes detect the cause from the report, but we should also give applicants the opportunity to explain the circumstances if they like.

192

The question isn't whether a candidate has flaws; it's whether we find them before we hire him.

Contrary to many résumés and first impressions, no candidate is perfect. Every applicant is some combination of quirks and faults, all of which will be obvious after a few months of work.

Most flaws aren't disqualifying in themselves except in their extremes—disorganization, inaccuracy, tardiness, slowness to start, sloppy dress, poor grammar, math deficiencies, etc. Every good candidate has some small mix of imperfections that are offset by his skills and positive traits.

Disqualifying flaws are led by dishonesty and theft, but also include poor motivation, unreliability, chronic absence, and inability to get along with customers and co-workers. Regardless of the underlying causes, making these people productive is beyond the scope and feasibility of most businesses.

Job candidates don't admit their shortcomings; indeed they do their best to conceal them. It's our responsibility to ferret them out, and that requires every skill and tool we can marshal—job application, credit check, criminal check, personal and job references, personality profile, multiple interviews ....

We live a long time with our hiring choices, and they reward or penalize us daily.

Hiring is an art that's never perfected, but it gives us lots of opportunities for learning and improving.

For some time we had key staff write out their predictions for new hires and put them in the employees' files.

After a few months we compared our predictions to performance. Sometimes we got the general prediction right, but every time there were personality traits and quirks we missed— occasionally critical ones. Then we reviewed the employees' job applications, notes from interviews, and personality projections to see what clues we should have gotten but missed.

Our conclusion was that our hiring skills and processes had much room for improvement, that there were almost always clues we could have picked up, and that no matter how thorough we were, we should have done more.

A trial period is not an alternative to careful hiring.

A trial period doesn't really make a hiring mistake easier to undo. Agreeing on an option date doesn't make releasing an employee any more pleasant for him, us, or his co-workers.

Nor does a trial period make a poor hire less expensive. The company pays the trial employee through his less-productive learning period and invests in his training, then must start over with another employee. Despite our original intentions, in most cases we simply keep the employees even when they aren't up to our standards.

Specifying a trial period makes little actual difference anyway, since either the employer or the employee can terminate most employment at any time. If one or both parties can see it's not working within a few days or weeks, there's little point in waiting for an option date.

Better to spend one day choosing carefully than ninety training and then firing.

194

Temporary work is the backdoor left unguarded.

Companies that use temp agencies rarely subject the temps to their usual hiring procedures—they simply call the agency and order an employee.

If the temp's work is satisfactory, the company often keeps them. Since their work is known, there's no need to go through applications and interviews. That means the new employee has effectively avoided all the company's standard hiring checks.

Despite their assurances, few temp agencies do thorough background checks—they deal with too many workers and for too short a time. If the candidate has experience and makes an acceptable impression, they try him on an assignment. If the first assignment is satisfactory, client feedback becomes his reference file.

Some people take temp work because they don't want full-time work; others like the variety. But many do temp work because they can't find full-time employment. And often the problem is something that comes to light in standard employment checks—previous job problems, criminal records, alcohol and drug abuse, mental instabilities, etc.

A temporary employee is still an employee. Before we let him inside our business and give him access to our inventory, assets, money, records, customers, and employees, all the standard checks and references should be run. The trouble and expense is negligible compared to the trouble and expense he can cause us.

Young people learn quickly, but leave quickly too.

Young fresh minds learn and adapt easily to new methods and technologies. That makes young people attractive candidates for high-tech and quickly evolving jobs, as well as temporary jobs like computer conversions, seasonal help, and special projects.

But for jobs that require long-term experience or have long learning curves, young people can be risky hires. They're necessarily exploring job options and fields, and realistically can't commit for the long term until they gather more experience. Their perspectives are shorter term, they often prioritize their social activities above work, and their personal lives are subject to sudden changes.

For jobs that require longevity, relationship building, or social interaction with more mature customers, older, more stable workers are usually better candidates.

196

Commissions are an empty promise to many job candidates.

Most job applicants are skeptical of sales commissions and many completely disregard them as part of compensation.

Some envision working days or weeks only to find the job doesn't pay what they need to live. Others worry about an occasional paycheck insufficient to meet bills. And most are familiar with cold-call sales jobs in which only extreme compensation can provide sufficient motivation to push past hostile receptions.

But commissions are also one of the few opportunities a job applicant has to earn more than market wages—indeed many commissioned employees earn multiples of what's available in hourly jobs. A good commission system offers a hard worker the opportunity to be paid in direct proportion to his efforts and effectiveness.

Nevertheless attracting good applicants to a commission sales job, regardless of its potential, is often challenging. Showing them the earnings of current employees can help reassure them, but in most cases we also have to offer a guarantee, at least for an initial period.

197

We can't have
too many good people.

Top-quality people find ways to be useful. They have skills, energy, intelligence, and enthusiasm that can turn virtually any reasonable opportunity into profit.

As a result we can almost always afford to hire these people whenever we find them—even when there's no obvious position available.

In most cases we need only give them some orientation in the company and explain the goals. Their natural drive will attract them to ways they can fit in and contribute.

198

A good salesman can sell almost any
product —but much more of a good product.

A good salesperson can be the solution to a slow-moving product or an underperforming department or location. In many cases they are the key to turning it around.

But good salespeople are rare and valuable. If we could get all of them we want, we'd gladly fill every position with them. Sadly, they're not so easy to find.

Those we do find are far more valuable to us and themselves talking to more customers, selling more profitable products, and pursuing bigger opportunities. (And that increased value allows us to pay them better and keep them longer.)

Unfortunately for our weaker products, departments, and locations, our best salespeople belong on our best opportunities.

Tell the job, don't sell it.

It's counterproductive to talk an applicant into a job he isn't suited for or might not like. He'll discover the truth soon enough and if it's not as expected he'll quit; both the company and the applicant will have wasted time and effort.

It's more practical to describe the job thoroughly and honestly, including all of its challenges, occasional disappointments and unpleasant situations (e.g., upset customers, unexpected schedules, conflicting priorities, stress, competitive pressures, etc.) If our description raises concerns, it's better to discuss them now than to discover them later.

Methods and customers belong to the store, not its employees.

It seems unfair that we could pay an employee to learn our methods and create relationships with our customers and he then take both to our competitor.

Fortunately the courts often agree—if we've specified it in an employment agreement.

A non-compete contract can prohibit employees from working for a direct competitor for a specified time period, usually 1-3 years, after they leave us.

Courts in some states enforce them erratically or not at all, but in other areas they're consistently upheld— we can stop an employee from working for a competitor and/or sue the competitor for interfering with our contract.

But perhaps the contracts' greatest value is not so much that they can be enforced but that they seldom have to be; employees who understand the contract when they sign it are usually reluctant to break it.

PERSONALITIES

201

Every head is a different world.

Each man's perception is his reality, and the differences can be astonishing. One person sees opportunity in what another perceives as danger. One senses a crowd as threatening while another is energized by the potential interaction. One welcomes change while another focuses only on what he'll give up. One views kidding as a sign of friendship while another perceives it as hostility and provocation.

Personality is the brain's filter and whatever information gets through is that person's world. If it's biased toward action and accomplishment, the individual is assertive and energetic. If it's biased toward emotion and feeling, the person is social and sympathetic. If it's biased toward blame, the individual is conservative and reserved.

I once sat in a roundtable discussion with a lady who made an enthusiastic proposal other participants didn't think much of. One of them stated it surprisingly clearly: "That's the stupidest idea I've ever heard." Most of us at the table were stunned to silence, but she never lost stride. "Yeah, and we could also ...," as if she'd just gotten a ringing endorsement.

I confess that I entertained all the unflattering scenarios that could have made her so oblivious. But soon it also occurred to me that such a positive outlook could, on occasion, be productive, and maybe I'd be lucky to have some of it rub off on me.

As strange and comical as her attitude and enthusiasm were to the rest of us, they were also infectious. Ultimately the group endorsed her (stupid) proposal. It's unlikely anyone else at that table could have accomplished that— nor would they have even tried.

Knowledge is irrelevant when the personality isn't right.

We can teach an employee many things—products, methods, systems ... even language, dress, and manners when necessary. But if they don't have the right personalities for the jobs we put them in, they simply can't produce the results we need.

Personality comes from deep within and is not a choice. Neither we nor an employee can change his personality to match a job.

Good salespeople won't do accurate paperwork— a constant source of irritation to their co-workers in accounting. But put the accounting people on the sales floor and there'll be little to account for. Technicians will be precise and accurate—and wonder what offends those they converse with. No amount of training, reasoning, rewarding, or threatening can change these things; it's not in them and we can't put it there.

An all-star team is all-star only when the players are in the correct positions.

> In all the great inspirational biographies, the hero's personality is never the obstacle but rather the prevailing force.

Customer experiences are the product of people skills.

Good people skills can turn difficult situations into compliments; poor people skills can turn agreeable situations into complaints.

Pleasant experiences are most often the result of making the customer feel welcome and important, even if products and services are less than they should be. Bad experiences, despite what the customer cites as the problem, are usually the result of making him feel slighted and unimportant.

The concept is simple, but its implementation is easy only to those with innate people skills.

For some years our band instrument repair shop was the sore point of our business. Despite excellent work, charging too little to cover our costs, reducing turnaround time almost to a day, and having two technicians inspect and sign off on every completed repair, we had to deal with one or more unhappy customers nearly every week.

We convinced ourselves that that was just the nature of repairs—customers would never be happy about incurring an expense they hadn't anticipated and for which they only got things back to their previous state.

Eventually, at the technicians' request, we hired a service manager; the technicians made the case that if they didn't have to talk to customers (which they didn't like doing) they could handle more work.

From the service manager's first day complaints virtually disappeared. His social personality allowed him to talk amiably with customers, help them understand the work needed, and make them feel appreciated.

Not only was everyone happier but prices could be increased to more reasonable levels.

Smart and talented are just the public face of determined and persistent.

Most people call a person who achieves impressive things smart. Indeed he does know what's needed to achieve his goals, but not because he was born with the information; he simply makes a point of learning what he needs when he needs it. He does what he has to do to get the results he wants.

In time, determination virtually always trumps unmotivated natural ability.

If we want to hire "smart" people, it's not an intelligence test we should give but a personality test.

Personality tests recognize before hiring what we recognize afterward.

It's nearly impossible to read a personality in a short conversation, especially a job interview where the applicant tries hard to project an image often much different from himself. Usually it takes us weeks or even months of working closely with someone to see his or her true colors—and by then it's difficult and expensive to correct mistakes.

Personality tests (or "surveys") are amazingly accurate indicators of job traits like sociability, patience, assertiveness, sense of urgency, attention-to-detail, and persistence. As a result these tests are surprisingly effective in predicting what jobs a person would be most successful in.

For the first twenty years of my retail career I equated personality surveys with astrological signs and palm reading. Eventually, when several retailers I respect recommended them, I decided to at least listen to the salesman.

He had no pitch; he simply asked me to have three employees fill out the one-page survey, and without meeting the people he interpreted their personalities.

"This is one of your top salesmen." He had my attention.

"This is probably a bookkeeper. He's consistent and dependable." Right again!

"This person is probably a technician, perhaps computers or instrument repair." Aha!! Wrong, he's a salesman.

"Well, he's not a very good one. Both of you would be happier if he were doing something more detailed and with less people interaction." Whoa! So that's why ...?!!!

Since that day we haven't hired a single person without a personality survey. Rarely has it missed.

206

Changing a personality is a futile wish.

It's useless to ask an employee to change a behavior that's imbedded in his personality. He might do his best to accommodate, but he'll quickly grow tired and revert to being himself.

Every employee eventually reaches a plateau indicative of his natural potential at his job. If he's a good match to the job, his performance will be much higher than average. If he's a poor match, his plateau will be a fraction of average.

As hard as we might try, we can't change him significantly or permanently. A personality isn't a choice or a learned skill, but a core definition. It's ingrained deep within, where we have only slight and fleeting influence.

Better to find the employee a job that fits his personality, and put a better fit into his job. In the long run everyone will be happier and more productive.

207

Talents in sales and paperwork are inversely related.

Good salespeople are notoriously poor at paperwork. Highly detailed people are notoriously poor at sales. Trying to combine the two is useless and will frustrate everyone.

Top quality salespeople are so rare and valuable, it often makes sense to expect and adapt to their paperwork shortcomings—despite the resentment this often causes in the back offices. In extreme cases it makes sense to have an accounting staffer take over as soon as the customer agrees to a purchase.

We can't treat them the same when they're not.

Treating everyone the same is an admirable philosophy based on the equality we all strive for. Only it doesn't work.

We can speak bluntly and directly to some employees; others require a soft touch, couching even gentle suggestions in affirmations. Some are motivated by our approval, some by teamwork, some by duty, some only by money—and some by nothing we can offer.

We learn how to interact and what responses to expect largely through trial and error. But an understanding of the personalities underlying those responses can reduce frustrations and improve communications.

PAY

209

Low wages aren't a bargain, good people are.

A low payroll is virtually always more than offset by low production, poor performance, mistakes, inefficiencies, lack of motivation, and poor retention.

Retail has no jobs for which the quality of the employee is unimportant. Top salespeople create high sales; poor salespeople waste opportunities. Good managers develop long-term employees; bad managers create turnover. Smart buyers find saleable products; poor buyers waste resources and accumulate dead stock. Skilled office workers provide timely and accurate information; less competent workers make mistakes that require hours to unravel and render information useless. Even a parking lot guard must be dependable, vigilant, and honest—hardly universal traits.

The bargain is not in paying less, but in employing better people.

210

It's not good people we can't afford, it's average people.

A good salesperson often sells two to three times what an average salesperson sells and builds a following of loyal customers. Can we afford to pay them more? You bet we can!

Differences in performance are just as great in other jobs but aren't always as obvious—sales are simply the easiest to measure.

Our objective is to attract people who do outstanding work, not people who are willing to work for the wages.

In our musical instrument business the difference between average, good, and outstanding salespersons looks like this:

	Average	Good	Outstanding
Sales	400,000	800,000	1,200,000
COGs	240,000	480,000	720,000
Margin	160,000	320,000	480,000
Payroll	40,000	65,000	90,000
PP margin	120,000	255,000	390,000

As you can imagine we're always on the lookout for outstanding salespeople and fight hard to keep them.

211

Employee retention is the best value in retailing.

Most retail jobs have long learning curves. (Many consumers probably doubt this, but their opinions are based on what the typical retail employee knows rather than what he *should* know.)

New employees in any position become profitable only after they learn their jobs and gain some experience. The tuition is high in mistakes, inefficiencies, overlooked opportunities, and trial and error (mostly on our customers)—and we, not they, pay it. Salespeople, particularly for high-end goods, often take a year to reach breakeven and two years or more to show their potential.

A good long-term employee is a treasure; losing one is a tragedy felt all the way to the bottom line.

Once, in a downturn, one of our local competitors resolved to hold down expenses by reducing the pay of his top salespeople. They didn't take this kindly, as might be expected, and inquired about opportunities with us.

I'm embarrassed to say that we debated for over a week whether we could afford them and how we could use them. Ultimately we recognized our good fortune, welcomed them with attractive offers, and made jobs for them.

They brought valuable relationships along with long-term experience. Our sales skyrocketed while our competitor's nosedived; within a year he was gone.

His simple misjudgment of the value of his people was tragic; it was impossible not to feel sorry for him (although our sympathy didn't extend to giving the people back).

It was probably the easiest and most profitable opportunity that ever fell in our laps, and we're eternally grateful that no one else scooped them up while we wasted so much time.

212

Having good people means paying more, but paying more doesn't mean having good people.

Better pay attracts and retains better workers. But it attracts and retains poor workers too, and they're even happier to work for the higher wages—so much so that they're unlikely to ever leave us voluntarily. Paying more assures only that their poor performance will be long-term unless we take action to weed them out.

In addition to paying more, to have better people we have to be selective in hiring and willing to move out those who don't meet our performance standards.

213

In business a man is equal only to his results.

Equal opportunity is an admirable goal; equal achievement is a naïve dream. We achieve according to our attitudes and efforts—and they are far from equal.

No reasonable law or moral code requires that employees be paid the same regardless of productivity. To the contrary, intelligent legislation, good business practice, and proper morals require that we judge and reward employees according to their performance and only their performance.

Employees occasionally misunderstand this. Their rationalization for a raise is sometimes that their expenses have gone up, or that they've been with the company another year. While these deserve our understanding and appreciation, they aren't in themselves reasons to give a raise.

We should reward performance, always and only, and make every effort to assure that employees are aware of that.

A good incentive system is management on autopilot.

Tying a portion of each person's pay directly to his results automatically rewards good performance and weeds out poor performance. Managers are relieved of the unpleasantness of riding herd and can focus instead on assisting team members in achieving mutual goals.

Good employees are motivated by the challenge of the incentives and appreciate the opportunity to control their pay. Those who don't respond to incentives are probably in the wrong jobs.

Straight commission is insecure and unfriendly; no commission is unproductive and unrewarding.

Sales commissions, the classic compensation system in retailing, can be any portion of total pay, from zero to 100 percent.

Some retailers feel that if commission incentivizes, straight commission incentivizes best. Others feel that any commission creates an unfriendly environment in which sales take too high precedence over customer service. Most find some middle ground most satisfactory.

Commissions should be high enough to ensure sufficient attention and efforts, but not so high as to make salespeople anxious about meeting their bills or uncooperative in efforts other than sales.

Twenty to fifty percent of total pay is usually enough to provide focus, although where high-quality/high-earning salespeople are critical, commissions might be as much as 75 percent of earnings, or even 100 percent backed by a guaranteed draw against future earnings.

A good balance between commission and wages pays those with high sales enough to retain and reward them, and encourages those with low sales to either improve their skills or move on to work more suitable to their abilities.

Non-salespeople deserve incentives too.

The production of salespeople is easy to measure and reward, but most other jobs have objectives that can be tracked and rewarded too.

Thinking through the objectives of a job usually makes potential incentives obvious. They could be based on quantities, such as invoices produced, packages shipped, receivables collected, etc. But other measurements are sometimes more appropriate—turnaround times, error rates, satisfaction surveys, inspection results, deadlines met, etc. The incentives can be earned individually or as a group.

(The use of incentives doesn't imply that employees respond only to their own self-interests. Incentives emphasize the team's objectives and are like the score in a ballgame. They provide feedback and a source of the accomplishment, respect, recognition, and teamwork that make work interesting and fun. When incentives are earned, the whole company benefits.)

217

Careful what you reward as that's what you'll get.

Incentives are strong determinants of focus and efforts, and consequently should be designed with care.

When employee incentives are correctly aligned with company objectives, the company and its employees share common goals and work smoothly together. When company goals and employee incentives don't match, company and employees work against each other.

If we pay only by hours worked, we convey to our people that showing up is important, but not necessarily producing. If we pay commissions on gross sales, we tell our salespeople that sales are the goal, but not that the sales should be profitable. If we pay by invoices processed or packages shipped, we convey that speed is valued but not necessarily accuracy.

It's not possible to include every objective in an incentive system and still keep it practical. We can only select those we value most and anticipate the challenges with the others.

They hear what you say, but they do what you pay.

Employees are generally eager to please management. They listen to everything the boss says, particularly about objectives and what they're expected to accomplish. They set out with determination to meet and exceed expectations—to make a real contribution to goals.

But too often they discover the job's incentives don't match the goals as management explained them. The result is not only confusion concerning the objectives but damage to management's credibility.

A manager's words resonate for a while and then fade. Incentives speak with every pay check.

He who says money isn't a good motivator doesn't know a good salesman.

Some motivational psychologists tell us money isn't a good motivator. Yes, there *are* people money doesn't motivate. Hopefully they don't work for us.

Good salespeople need a determination and drive that is rarely provided by any other focus or reward than money. The best salespeople typically have expensive tastes—fancy cars, large houses, fashionable clothes, impressive jewelry. They're rarely without another acquisition in their sights if not already on their credit cards, and consequently are always hungry for the next sale.

Some have said the attraction is not the income itself but rather its reflection of the score. That's apparently the case with many wealthy business people. Good salespeople seem to enjoy the competition and the respect of winning. But a win is a win only when they make money.

A good salesperson is the high expense we want.

A high-paid, high-selling salesperson is more profitable than an average salesman often simply because his payroll is a smaller percentage of his sales and gross margins.

But he brings other advantages, too. The good salesman often talks to the same number of customers as the average salesman; he just sells to more of them—he's more efficient with the customers the store attracts. His sales are also usually "cleaner," resulting in fewer returns and better customer satisfaction. And he provides good example to the other salespeople.

The high pay of a top salesperson shouldn't be a concern when it's within an acceptable percentage of his sales and gross margins. More often it's a bargain.

A commission system is an unfriendly environment only to those who don't want to do business.

Some retailers shun commissions; they believe they can create a more helpful, comfortable, and lower-pressure environment for their customers when salespeople aren't on commission.

It's true that non-commissioned salespeople are less concerned with whether a customer buys—but does that mean they're helpful? Commissioned salespeople are focused on matching the customer to the right product, explaining its benefits, and facilitating the sale. Those who come to buy consider that helpful.

Some customers with no intention of buying *do* appreciate a non-commissioned environment; they can be comfortable whiling away their day with our salespeople. Meanwhile those who want to buy are put off and frustrated by the lack of attention and focus.

When prices are negotiable, commissions must be based on profit.

Calculating commissions as a percentage of sales just doesn't work when salespeople have to negotiate prices; the incentive to make sales regardless of margin is in direct conflict with maintaining the gross margins the store needs to operate.

Some stores attempt to keep negotiable pricing within bounds by requiring that every deal be approved by a manager. This pits the employee and customer against management, is demotivating for employees, and is an operational bottleneck.

Basing commissions on gross profit, despite its complications, is one of the few ways to keep negotiable pricing in line with company needs.

Pay is the secret everyone knows.

The idea that pay is a private agreement between employer and employee sounds good and makes sense; it just doesn't work.

Pay information is just too enticing and there are too many ways to discover it for it to stay secret long.

Telling employees not to tell other employees what they make only means precede it with "Don't tell the boss I told you." The result is often dissatisfied and distrustful employees who can't tell you what's bothering them.

Better to assume pay will be discussed or at least discovered, maintain consistency, and keep channels of communication open.

It's not the money difference that upsets them, but their placement on the scale.

Employees' irresistible interest in what other employees make is not so much in what they could do with the difference as in management's relative scale of worth. Regardless of whether all employees are overpaid or underpaid, perceived discrepancies in the scale create hard feelings.

Since everyone understands his or her own work and dedication better than that of others, some discontent is inevitable and just the lot of management. Consistency according to our own judgment is the best we can do.

A change in pay can only be a raise.

Tinkering with a pay agreement is sensitive business, regardless of the logic or fairness. Any change that is or might be perceived as a pay reduction is tantamount to breaking a promise or stealing a possession.

When hiring, we're free to offer any amount and terms we like. But renegotiating afterwards is considered a violation of trust and good faith—unless of course it's a raise.

Charge-backs are never "fair."

When sales are voided due to returns, non-payment, etc., charging the commission back to the salesperson almost always causes resentment and hard feelings. Regardless of the reason, salespeople tend to rationalize its unfairness.

A commission system structured to avoid charge-backs (e.g., pays commissions only after payment clears) creates less ill will. And for the remaining situations that arise, it's often better to absorb the loss than to stir up acrimony.

(Some will no doubt disagree with this philosophy as unfair in itself. Hopefully they'll recall that disagreements and animosity are rarely based on absolute fairness, but on individual perspectives, biased and rationalized by personal interests. "Absolute fairness" is often as counterproductive as blurting out every fact that crosses one's mind because "it's true." Occasional generosity is often more helpful in maintaining positive working relationships than exacting interpretations of "fairness.")

In payroll mistakes
only underpayments are correctable.

It's usually not possible to recover an accidental over-payment in payroll without creating hard feelings.

Unless the amount is large, it's typically better to point out the mistake to the employee and explain that you're letting it go; then ensure the mistake doesn't recur in future payrolls.

(However, if the mistake was significant enough to be apparent to the employee and he chose not to report it, more important than recovery is whether we want this person on staff.)

Requests for a raise are opportunities
to negotiate improvements.

Discussions of raises can be welcomed and focus turned to potential improvements in performance: "Let's talk about how you're doing and what you might do to increase your value to the company. Maybe we can find a way to accomplish what you have in mind."

(Employees who are on commission don't need to ask for a raise, but the discussion can still be worthwhile.)

TRAINING

Training doesn't cost, it pays.

Training is an investment with guaranteed returns—increased efficiency, better organization, improved reliability, more satisfied customers, more successful employees, etc.

Trained salespeople produce more sales than untrained salespeople. Customers appreciate their knowledge, listen to their recommendations, sense their conviction, and respond to their confidence. They buy from them and are grateful for their help.

Employee training is retailing's easiest competitive advantage.

Retail employees are notoriously untrained. Who hasn't encountered a retail employee who knew almost nothing about his products and didn't seem to care? Many shoppers would say they're more rule than exception.

Which makes training one of the greatest opportunities in retailing. Standing above our competitors is easy; we simply have to train our people—on products, salesmanship, systems, methods, customer interaction, display, merchandising, and anything else that matters in the operation of our businesses.

Experimenting on our customers is the training we can't afford.

We know the value of training, but unfortunately it rarely fits into the real-world schedule of retailing. We don't find out about job openings weeks in advance; when we're lucky enough to get a two-week notice, it typically takes that long to find an acceptable candidate. By the time we get the new hire aboard, the shortage of personnel is wearing employees and customers thin. So we press new employees into service, assigning other salespeople to give them what amounts to little more than an orientation. They learn by the most expensive training method we can devise—experimenting on our customers.

Most of us are painfully aware of the irony. We've invested in all the other expenses of our businesses—rent, fixtures, inventory, systems, advertising …. We get the customer into the store, if not ready and willing to buy, at least with interest. And then the salesperson doesn't know the questions to ask, the products to show, the recommendations to make, or the features and benefits to explain. His lack of confidence is contagious, and only the most determined customers buy.

The cost is frightening. Training is a bargain in comparison.

Training is an employee benefit.

Employees like training. They want to learn the skills, be knowledgeable and effective, and have information and expertise to offer their customers. They like to be appreciated by their customers, respected by their peers, and valued by management. Everyone enjoys doing things they're good at.

Participating in well-executed training isn't a dreaded chore but a privilege. It inspires salespeople and creates enthusiasm for products and selling. It increases sales, incomes, employee satisfaction, and customer appreciation.

Salespeople sell what they know.

Salesmen like to show products they understand and appreciate. They enjoy sharing their knowledge, and they demonstrate enthusiasm for products they believe in.

Their attraction to a product is not so much its superiority but rather their understanding of its features and how they can benefit the user.

One of the most effective ways to enhance sales of a product is to teach the salespeople about it. Smart retailers (and smart manufacturers) understand this and provide training at every opportunity.

> We once hired a young guitar salesman who was enamored with a guitar we didn't carry. The brand, Rickenbacker, enjoyed a good reputation, mostly the result of its use by the Beatles' George Harrison, but the Beatles' heyday was past and the guitar's European origin made it expensive; as a consequence few were being sold in the U.S.
>
> We trained him thoroughly on the products we stocked and he became an excellent salesman. But he didn't forget the Rickenbacker brand, and when he had accumulated prepaid orders for several we relented and agreed to stock a few.
>
> Over the next year he sold so many Rickenbackers that the national sales manager came to see what he was doing. What he found was simply a salesman who knew the product well, believed in it, and loved to tell his customers about it.

New hires are eager to learn; don't make them wait.

New employees are excited about their new jobs and want to learn what they'll need to do the job well.

They're willing to invest the time if we simply give them the information.

There's no reason to make them wait, even for their first day of work. If we have the material organized and prepared, we can give it to them immediately when they're hired. They can come to work with a head-start that benefits both them and the store.

Write it once, teach it forever.

We need our training information over and over again, many times in the long term. It makes sense to collect and organize it, in notebooks, manuals, or digital files.

Training materials don't have to be formal or fancy—just a collection of our thoughts and ideas, or even literature and articles written by others. We can add to it whenever we think of something new or come across something worthwhile; employees and managers can be encouraged to add their thoughts.

Good product manuals should include an overview of product construction, brief backgrounds on the major manufacturers, a glossary of product terms, product price points, and a list of models with features and benefits. But they can also include competitors' products, features, and pricing, the shortcomings of non-standard products, an explanation of product accessories and their uses, a list of appropriate add-ons, and more.

Sales literature, manufacturer training materials, and product articles are a good place to start. They can simply be punched and added to a notebook. Or they can be scanned into a document that can be added to, refined, and printed out as needed.

A personnel manual
makes a strong start.

Personnel manuals typically cover basics like hours, dress, parking, vacations, holidays, employee purchases, benefits, sexual harassment, and obligatory employment notices. But they can also include anything we feel will help an employee get his or her bearings quickly: company history, philosophies, an organizational chart, a roster of personnel (with pictures) and their responsibilities, an overview of activities, basic operational methods ....

Writing a personnel manual isn't difficult—it's mostly writing down the policies we've already established. If some of our policies need to be clarified, this is a good time to do it. Add to this the background and instructions we regularly give new employees.

Model personnel manuals are available in libraries, bookstores, and on the Internet, and many commercially available software programs make writing them quick and painless.

A manual is not a literary work.

Our manuals shouldn't be formal; a strict literary style intimidates staffers who might otherwise contribute.

We can just write it as we would say it. The goal is simply to collect and share information, ideas, and techniques that have proven useful. The most helpful information is often what we and our staff contribute from experience.

Writing a manual isn't the insurmountable task it might seem. Most of the information is already in our stores and needs only to be gathered and organized. As time allows, staff can add background and the information can be organized into text, charts, and lists.

Once a manual is put in use, new information accumulates quickly and the manual evolves into a comprehensive training document specific to our situations and products.

Contribution creates commitment.

Those most qualified to write, or at least contribute to, a store's manuals are its employees. They're on the front line and have firsthand knowledge. They're also reminded daily of what else is needed and can easily make note of new information and methods they come across.

Being asked to participate in the creation of a manual should be an honor since it recognizes in-depth knowledge and expertise. Employees develop more commitment to both the manuals and their purpose when their ideas are included.

Writing a manual makes an expert.

Nothing refines and reinforces an idea like writing it out. Expressing it clearly and concisely requires collecting and reviewing details, examining them for accuracy, considering alternate viewpoints, and selecting accurate phrasing.

A salesperson who doesn't know a product as well as he should is a good candidate for writing that section of the manual. The process of learning and writing will turn him into an authority in both knowledge and recognition. After all, he wrote the book.

Customers, employees, and managers love certifications.

Certifications are a win for everyone. Employees are motivated to learn, take pride in being certified, and are more confident in their work. Customers like knowing that the employee has proven expertise, appreciate and take advantage of the increased knowledge, and are more comfortable and trusting in the employees' recommendations. And managers know that when salespeople are trained and tested, sales increase, customers are better served, and complaints are reduced.

If it's important to know, certify that it's known.

Salesmanship and product knowledge are essential training, but many other aspects of retailing can benefit from training and certification as well—display, security, handling complaints, accounting, inventory control, computer software, telephones, purchasing, management, repair, delivery, etc. Whatever is important for smooth operation of the store can and should be certified.

Certification can be as simple as a written test, or it can include an oral exam, role-playing, videotaping, a written assignment, etc.

Employees should be allowed and encouraged to pass the certification levels as soon as they learn the information—the sooner the better. This not only encourages them to increase their effectiveness quickly but also creates motivation by giving them control over their careers and advancement.

Recognition is motivation.

Certifications can be presented at store meetings and should be in front of as many people as possible. The ceremony can be serious or fun, but praise for the accomplishment should be sincere. Those who previously achieved the certification can be recognized also—"She joins the distinguished company of …"—reinforcing the value we put on certification and encouraging others to join the group.

Framable certificates are easy and inexpensive to create and provide a source of pride as well as notification to customers. Acknowledgments of certifications (e.g., "Woodwind Certified") can be added to the employee's name tag, business cards, and stationery—all of which can be printed inexpensively in-house.

A large plaque or display board on the sales floor can acknowledge all employee certifications with individual engraved name plates under each category.

Hanging framed employee bios in each area of the sales floor helps customers get to know the salespeople and provides a simple and effective way to advertise their expertise.

When they learn, confer a degree.

Those who achieve various levels of certifications can be recognized by granting them degrees—associate, bachelor, masters, and doctorate.

A commencement ceremony including presentation of a diploma, possibly followed by a graduation party, is both fun and significant recognition. Announcements and pictures make good publicity in a newsletter, the company website, and occasionally even the local newspaper.

Training incentives
determine training priorities.

Certifications become priorities when incentives are attached. For example, the right to earn commissions might be contingent on salesmanship certification. If there are levels of certification, the commission rates might increase with each level.

Certain products might require certification before commissions can be earned on their sales. Or salespeople might be given priority access to customers for these products.

Other certifications might be rewarded with an increase in hourly wages or other benefits. Management certification can be required of employees who want to move up.

Training is a process,
not an event.

Training is never complete. New products are introduced, technology improves, techniques get rusty, competitors change strategies, customer expectations evolve, we find better ways ....

As a result training must be continuous to keep ourselves and our staffs up-to-date and in peak selling condition.

In addition to independent training with manuals, books, videos, and certifications, group training can consist of regular meetings that include presentations, demonstrations, contests, brainstorming sessions, discussion of articles and videos, and other activities.

The training schedule must be sacred.

Training meetings must be regular—preferably a set day and time each week. When the schedule isn't fixed, meetings are pre-empted by more pressing but less important activities and training becomes just another good idea we don't get to.

Meetings should be separated by topic and only the relevant staff invited. There can be salesmanship meetings (just salesmen), product meetings (only the staff that deals with that particular product), service meetings, credit and collection meetings, etc., in addition to operational meetings for the whole store.

247

Speakers and topics are more abundant than time.

Sources of sales meeting material are plentiful. Good manufacturers' reps welcome the opportunity to show and teach the benefits of their products. Trade associations usually have selections of high quality videos and books. Almost every city has a Dale Carnegie Institute and other organizations with professional trainers. Training books and videos are abundant in bookstores, on the Internet, and in libraries.

The most relevant training
is conducted by the staff itself.

Outside trainers are rarely necessary. Our employees know what information and skills are most helpful, and sharing responsibility for meeting content creates buy-in.

The best meetings are participative, ideally with each attendee leading some aspect. Activities can include: discussing recent situations, successes, and challenges; sharing staff knowledge and expertise; presenting outlines of products' features and benefits; reviewing systems and methods; brainstorming improvements; comparing experiences with sales techniques; sharing methods of customer follow-up; role-playing common situations (especially creating rapport, sales objections, price negotiations, and handling complaints); viewing and voting on submitted videos of product demonstrations (with a substantial prize to the winner); examining and comparing competitors' products; contests for the highest number of follow-up calls; and reviewing customer feedback.

The trainer learns the most.

Assigning a staff member to conduct training on a product or technique often benefits the trainer more than the staff. He learns the material, solidifies commitment, and becomes an expert and advocate.

If no one on staff is knowledgeable about a new or important product, we can assign it to someone to learn and present. He can get the information with a little effort and research. The presentation creates a deadline and ensures the product will be learned thoroughly—no one wants to appear unprepared or incompetent to his peers.

Role-playing is experience made affordable.

Role-playing is acting out a situation (e.g., you are the salesperson and your co-worker is the customer).

Employees can simulate common sales scenarios, difficult customers, tricky questions, tough negotiations, or any challenging situation. After a few rounds of role-play, the real world can serve up little we haven't seen and aren't prepared to cope with.

Video is the rare opportunity to see ourselves as our customers see us.

Salespeople who video themselves are always surprised by what they see. Typically they resolve to immediately change aspects of their appearance, demeanor, mannerisms, speech, or wording.

Telling them how they look doesn't have the same effect nor result in the same commitment to improve—seeing ourselves for ourselves is an educational experience with no substitute.

A contest in which each person videos himself in a mock sales situation or presentation adds some fun. The presentation voted best by the participants wins. Creating an entry for this contest usually requires much more time than contestants expect—mostly because they don't like what they see, change it, and re-record, often multiple times. Significant prizes can help maintain enthusiasm through the process.

Phone inquiries are predictable and so should be the answers.

A phone call is frequently our first, and sometimes our only, contact with a potential buyer. The answers we give determine whether we get a shot at the sale.

Most phone inquiries are similar in nature—we can probably put together a list of questions that encompasses 80 percent of the calls we get. And with a little thought, we can plan ideal responses.

A contest using a mystery caller serves as an incentive to learn and practice our responses, and a prize makes it fun. Comparing our calls to those of our competitors allows our salespeople to decide (pretty accurately) who will get the sale.

Factory training is expertise at the source.

For learning specific products, there's no better way than attending manufacturer-sponsored training sessions, especially at the factory.

Travel is expensive and covering for the missing employee is a hardship. But the salesperson virtually always sells enough of the product to create a nice return on investment—usually within days of return.

If you have the books,
open a library.

A library of books, software, videos, and audio files can be used over and over for many years. Employees can check the materials out, watch the videos at home or on their lunch hours, listen to the audios in their cars, and read the books in their spare time.

As for selecting materials, we can let the salespeople choose, reimbursing them for materials they buy and use, and adding the materials to the company library.

255

Good people management is an attitude, not a technique.

The wide gulf between good and bad managers is really one simple perception: good managers understand that people are not only willing to work, but want to be on the team and contribute to its goals.

That attitude more than any other characteristic or ability defines the world's inspirational and effective managers. They treat their people like willing, capable, and valuable team members, and they help them get involved and contribute.

When the manager has the right attitude, employees not only give their best efforts but love their work (and their manager).

In an adult recreational basketball league, players run and jump as long as their lungs and legs allow, fight for rebounds and loose balls, cover themselves in sweat, and exert themselves to the point of exhaustion. They yell, cheer, and exchange high fives, celebrate their wins, and mourn their losses.

Why? The game pays nothing—in most cases they have to pay to play. All they get is sore muscles and dirty clothes. Yet they replay the games in their minds, relive (and brag about) their good plays, and eagerly await the next game.

Because they want to be on a team, work toward a goal, participate in the challenges, and enjoy the respect and recognition of a job well done. That's enough to generate extraordinary effort.

Managers don't create motivation —employees bring it.

New employees are excited about their jobs. They're eager to learn their parts, hone their knowledge and skills, make their contributions, and become valuable team members.

We don't create that motivation; employees have it on their first day. Our role is simply not to kill it.

We explain the objectives to them, assure that they get the necessary training and tools, provide ongoing information and feedback, and recognize and respect their efforts and contributions. When we do that well, their enthusiasm and commitment build with their abilities, and they're able to play increasingly important roles.

> "A company's most important assets walk out the door every evening; the manager's job is to make sure they come back the next day."
>
> **—Bill McCormick, Jordan Kitts Music**

Players need to see the scoreboard too.

Effective managers share goals so all employees can participate in their achievement. "Here's what we're trying to accomplish …. This is how we can work together to make it happen …. Here's your part …. This is why it's important to all of us …. This is how we'll judge how we're doing …."

We tell them the rules of the game, share the strategy, give them a position to play—and let them see the score.

We struggle with how much information we should share—what employees really need to know and what's too sensitive to let out. Yes, there's a proper balance. But we rarely get close to it and always err on the side of too little. Not much information is really as sensitive as we think, and our employees are more committed and understanding than we imagine.

Motivated employees find ways; unmotivated employees find excuses.

Our motivated employees take pride in what they accomplish. They're constantly on the lookout for ways to do their work faster and better. They feel their responsibilities are important and they fight to achieve the goals they share with us and their co-workers.

An unmotivated employee doesn't care whether the work gets done. He does only what he has to do to avoid reprimand and looks for ways to reduce his workload. If his attitude gets bad enough, he can even direct his efforts to sabotage of management and the company—sometimes for amusement, but often as revenge for respect he feels he's been denied or injustices he feels he's suffered.

Why is a mighty motivator.

Some people will do things because they're told to, but it's usually half-heartedly and with shortcuts. The rest of us have long traditions of rejecting every "supposed to" until we prove its value for ourselves. (Tuition at the hard-knocks school is often high, but its lessons are more convincing.)

It's difficult for any of us to be committed to a cause we don't understand and appreciate. Once we comprehend its importance and potential consequences, we muster far more energy and ingenuity.

> A lumberjack was once offered the chance to double his hourly pay by turning his axe over and hitting the wood with the blunt side. Since he deemed the physical labor the same, he gladly accepted and celebrated his increase in pay. But by the end of the day he asked to return to his old arrangement because, he said, he just had to see the chips fly.

The best management style is your own.

There is no prototype management style for us to copy, no best manager to emulate, no ideal voice and inflection to rehearse, no set responses and reactions to practice in the mirror.

Great managers fill the spectrums from sensitive to gruff, introverted to gregarious, quiet to loquacious, coarse to refined. Whatever their styles, their staffs learn them like a language and their meanings and intentions are soon clear.

Being someone else is hard work and few of us are good enough actors for a convincing performance. Our employees would sense our exertion, awkwardness, and insincerity.

Fortunately for us our most convincing, agreeable, and effective styles are our own.

To get respect
give respect.

We like people who like us. We agree with their taste, bask in their admiration, and enjoy being with them. We understand and empathize with them, like to see them happy, and welcome opportunities to help them.

We dislike people who don't like us. Their failure to understand and appreciate our abilities, knowledge, interests, and accomplishments makes them unworthy of our friendship. Time with them is unpleasant so we try to avoid them. We have no inclination to help them; better to see them fail—and sometimes we can help them fail.

There is something to respect in everyone. If we have trouble finding it, we can let them help us. "Tell me about yourself," is a reliable beginning.

Showing respect is simple and inexpensive—phrasing communication politely, taking the time to listen and understand their viewpoints, recognizing their abilities and contributions, offering a word of appreciation, etc.

An old English proverb says, "Civility costs nothing."

Treat them as if they are
what you want them to become.

When employees disappoint, badgering and scolding seldom accomplish desired results; usually they backfire into bad attitude, poor self-image, and rebellion. Better to reinforce positive behaviors and think of less desirable behaviors as temporary and uncharacteristic.

Our people like us when we have high opinions of them and they're proud when they live up to our expectations.

> To make a person thoughtful, respect his thoughts; to make him trustworthy, show him trust; to make him responsible, give him responsibility.

90% of employees believe
they're in the top 10% of performers.

Since this seems unlikely, test it on a sample of employees. But don't share the results—they won't be motivating.

Perhaps this phenomenon is due to each employee understanding his own efforts and their importance better than those of his coworkers.

Whatever the explanation, we do well to anticipate it, as any indication that our assessment of them is less than their own can be devastating.

##

Employees treat customers as managers treat employees.

Attitude and tone emanate from the top. They filter down gradually and often imperceptibly, but their ultimate effect is undeniable: people treat others as they are treated.

If we're tough, cold, rule-bound, and uncaring with our employees, our customers will get the same treatment. And our employees will believe they have done exactly as we expect—indeed as we would have done ourselves.

265

Asking someone to do something because he does it well is more compliment than command.

The phrasing of a request determines in large part the enthusiasm with which it's executed. When we acknowledge abilities we make our requests almost irresistible.

"Sally, you did a nice job resolving Mr. Braxton's problem last week. Would you call this customer and see if you can help him with something similar?" is likely to evoke a better effort than "Sally, help this customer, please."

But the compliment must be sincere; if not, it will back-fire as manipulation.

> "A gentle word, a kind look, a good-natured smile can work wonders and accomplish miracles. There is a secret pride in every human heart that revolts at tyranny. You may order and drive an individual, but you cannot make him respect you."
>
> **—William Hazlitt**

Responsibility is an honor and reward, not a chore or burden.

Just as every ballplayer wants to be in the game, every employee wants to be in charge of something, to prove what he can do, and be recognized and respected for his contributions and successes. No one wants to sit idly, be "help," or handle busy-work for someone else who makes all the decisions and gets all the credit.

Responsibility makes work challenging, interesting, fun, and fulfilling. Giving responsibility is recognition, endorsement of abilities, and an expression of trust. It encourages staff to stay and sometimes even makes up for pay that might not be as high as elsewhere.

A manager's job isn't commanding but assisting.

Despite the popular misconception, a manager's role isn't telling his employees what to do. If he has chosen good people, trained them sufficiently, and explained the objectives clearly, the employees know what's to be done. They need only the opportunity to do it.

The manager's responsibility is to remove obstacles. He ensures that employees have sufficient information, effective tools, efficient and reliable systems, appropriate materials, and accurate feedback.

A fair method with enthusiasm gets better results than a proven method without ownership.

Sometimes telling an employee how to do his job is just irresistible. It seems such a waste of time and effort to let him do it any other way than the one we've already proven.

The employee would, of course, follow our instructions. But not with the commitment that comes with understanding or the pride and dedication that comes with making one's own decisions and improvements.

In most cases the best way to do something is the way the doer believes he should. Thus we often get better results when we give him some latitude in his methods than when we give precise instructions. Even if he doesn't come up with the most efficient method, his commitment usually more than makes up for the inefficiencies, and his increased understanding and confidence will find future applications. Besides, who's to say he can't find a better way, especially after he gets some experience in the job?

When his method is likely to create expensive problems, we can help him without quashing his ownership: "Here's a problem you're likely to encounter. I'll show you a way we've found to avoid it."

Compliments, recognition, and titles are management's greatest values.

It costs nothing but a little time to tell a co-worker he's done a good job. Yet it can improve his attitude and enthusiasm for a day, a week—sometimes a lifetime.

Recognizing him for a special achievement, an unusual ability, or an important role in the company boosts his pride and inspires him to contribute more. There are many opportunities for such recognition: in meetings, in memos or newsletters, while making introductions, or just during casual conversation.

Giving him a title that recognizes his special responsibilities or abilities creates recurring opportunities for him to be proud of his work; it reinforces his value to the company and gives him clout in dealing with customers and vendors.

Every Saturday morning we take nominations and vote for an MVP, outstanding customer service provider, and a salesman of the week. Each winner gets an inscribed award (a pen, calculator, business card case, or coffee mug) and is announced in the meeting minutes with the nominator's account of what he did.

Each month an Ambassador of the Month is voted from the winners; he parks in the Ambassador's parking place, gets $50 to take his spouse to dinner, and his picture is displayed in the hall for a year.

It's not the value of the trinket or prize that motivates but the nomination, discussion, and recognition; they're powerful encouragement and conveyors of common values.

Success deserves credit, failure benefit of the doubt.

When things go well, we should assume it was according to an employee's plan and due to their efforts. We can assign credit generously, congratulate them on what they did to achieve it, and recognize and praise their efforts and abilities.

When things don't go so well, we should avoid any appearance of looking for a scapegoat. If we don't understand something they did, we have to assume they have information we don't. We should take for granted that everyone gave his/her best effort, praise aspects that were done well, and together look for ways to do it better next time.

(This doesn't mean we should be oblivious to poor efforts. When a team member proves he doesn't share the team's goals or isn't willing to put forth the effort, we have to remove him ASAP.)

> "If thou art a master, sometimes be blind; if a servant, sometimes be deaf."
>
> **—Thomas Fuller**

Their successes are yours too.

Assuming we hired and trained our people, their accomplishments are direct reflections on us and our abilities.

We need to let them know we believe in them, we're pulling for them, and we're proud of them. "Congratulations! That's an impressive achievement. But I'm not surprised—I knew you'd be good at that."

> "A leader takes a little more than his share of the blame, a little less than his share of the credit."
>
> **—Arnold Glasgow**

Better to ask some of the questions than know all of the answers.

Old school management holds that the manager is the great repository of information and knows the most about every job. He was made manager because he has experience and proven abilities. His job now is to ensure that the people "under him" do their jobs the way he knows they should be done.

Perhaps that worked in factories in the early days of industrialization but today it's outdated, ineffective, and offensive.

A great conductor can't play every instrument in the orchestra, and probably none of them as well as the musicians he conducts. But he can organize and guide them into a coordinated performance and an interpretation of the music the audience will appreciate and enjoy.

A smart manager doesn't expect to be better at every job than the people who are doing them daily. His goal is to attract and train people who can do their jobs well—and if they do them better than he could, it's a tribute to his management.

Acknowledging people's experience and skills by asking their opinions and advice encourages pride in their work and increases their commitment. And it leads to better solutions, since no one understands a problem as well as those who deal with it directly.

> The wise manager hires the best man he can find for the job, gives him the tools he needs to do it, and then gets out of his way while he does it.

Disagreement is inevitable but being disagreeable isn't.

A manager can't agree with everything that's said and done. When systems aren't being followed, tasks aren't getting done, or work needs improvement, it's the manager's responsibility to remedy the problem.

The message to be conveyed often isn't inspiring but it doesn't have to be confrontational. Phrased positively it can express a helpful and constructive spirit.

"We've got a problem with .... Let's talk about how we can solve it."

Anger, impatience, and disrespect are counterproductive and almost always irreparably damage the relationship.

Minimum force is maximum motivation.

Great managers get outstanding results without being overbearing. Their reticence to resort to authority and threats shows a true respect for their people's abilities and motives and encourages them to willingly follow him.

When we hire people with the correct motivation and give them the information, training, and tools to do their jobs, they don't need us over their shoulders. They can make most decisions and handle most situations themselves. Letting them do it builds enthusiasm, commitment, and pride.

> "Influence is like a savings account. The less you use it, the more you've got."
>
> **—Andrew Young**

Listen long enough and they'll offer the solution.

Despite what they say, employees often don't want us to give them answers to the questions they ask. Many times they've already thought out the problem and know the solution—often better than we do, especially when we're caught off-guard and lack the context. Sometimes they just want confirmation; other times they're proud of their solution and want us to recognize it.

Blurting out an answer seems time efficient, but its benefits are short term. Employees need to collect information, think through the processes and issues, and develop confidence in their own judgment.

"I don't know. What do you think?" is often an ideal response. If their suggestion is reasonable, "Sounds right to me." If they're off base, "I'd worry that ....
What do you think about...?"

Employees who have knowledge and can exercise good judgment are far more valuable than those who memorize routines and limited scripts we give them.

A man who can't make mistakes can't make decisions.

A person who can't afford a mistake can never reach his full potential. He's cautious and afraid in his work, and consequently slower than average. He can't improve his methods, develop new skills and abilities, and increase his value to the company because he can't try anything new.

Employees need to know it's OK to make an occasional mistake—no one will reprimand or embarrass them for it.

When mistakes happen, the employee usually knows what he did and how to avoid it next time; calling more attention to it serves no useful purpose. If someone needs help in recognizing or resolving a problem, we can usually find a way to offer it as constructive assistance accompanied by reassurance and encouragement.

> We once had an older employee who, despite continual training, refused to use the computers because she was afraid of making a mistake. Eventually we told her when she made her first mistake we would buy lunch for everyone in her department—and we did. With the encouragement of her coworkers, she became not an expert, but at least a proficient computer user.

They hear what you say but they see what you do.

The strongest guidance we give is through example. When it clashes with what we preach, our actions are presumed our real values and our words, past and future, lose their credence.

If we tell our people it's important to be on time, we also must arrive on time (preferably early), stay within our allotted time for lunch, and work to or past our scheduled ending times. If we encourage accurate and timely paperwork, we must maintain our own records impeccably and according to the systems we've established. When we preach reasonable margins and suggesting add-ons, we should minimize our own discounting and habitually show the extra products.

When our words and actions match, the combination is a powerful illustration and endorsement of not only our processes but our credibility.

278

Trust takes years to build, minutes to destroy.

For our employees to have confidence in how we'll treat them in the future we have to demonstrate consistent fairness over many individual situations. One instance of unpredictability or perceived unfairness will forever haunt a relationship.

This means not only *being* fair with everyone—customer, employee, vendor—in every situation, but occasionally exceeding our own interpretation of fairness to meet others' perceptions.

When we promise an employee something for the future (a raise, increased responsibility, a bonus, recognition, etc.), we should add it to our calendar or to-do list; forgetting is simply not an acceptable excuse, and reneging is a sure way to destroy trust.

If we lie to a customer or vendor, those who witness it will assume it's our standard operating procedure with everyone. If we exaggerate earnings to lure a potential hire, we only bring a dissatisfied and distrustful employee into the company where his distrust will be contagious.

Our word is our bond; changing our minds, forgetting, falling short, reneging, and especially deception are simply not options.

> Those who believe dishonesty is inherent in business know far less of the ways of the world than they like to believe.

Employees aren't interruptions of our duties, they are our first duty.

The manager who complains that too much of his time is taken by people has a dangerous misunderstanding of his role.

As business managers, we choose either to stay small and do the work ourselves or to grow by hiring and managing people. If we choose people, our first responsibility is assuring they have everything they need to do their work; only after we've done that should we take on tasks of our own.

Managing people takes time. They need tools, knowledge, systems, encouragement, feedback, and reassurance. Channels of communication must be kept open; issues and problems need to be discussed, philosophies and systems coordinated, and respect and recognition conveyed. When we rush any of these, we limit the contribution our people can make as well as create resentment and animosity.

A cavalry troop came across a hilltop to find its advance scout lying on the ground beside his horse, both shot full of arrows.

When the commander exclaimed, "We were just across the hill!!! Why didn't you call for us?!" the scout muttered, "Couldn't. Too busy fighting Indians."

The closer you are to the top the less you hear of the truth.

Few if any employees feel they can be completely open with the boss. As a result much of the "common knowledge" in our companies would come as a complete surprise to us.

Rumors, tiffs between employees, romantic and sexual relationships, mistakes, dissatisfaction, plans to leave, opinions of managers, legal and financial problems, and personal challenges are, by unspoken understanding, off-limits to us.

I once went to a 50th birthday party for one of our long-time employees. Many of our co-workers and their spouses were there, but I didn't see the man's wife. When I asked, "Where's Debbie?" the room got quiet and people looked at each other as if to say, "Uh oh. Who's going to answer this ugly question?" Finally the man said, "Debbie and I have been separated for some years now." As the evening went on I gathered that one of the ladies at the party was unofficially filling the role.

Later he felt obligated to explain that he hadn't mentioned the separation to me, despite our working together for over twenty years, because he wasn't proud of the reasons for it. From the silence and embarrassment my question brought to the party it was clear that I was the only one who didn't know—and still don't know the "reasons."

But then who would tell such things to their boss?

281

Leave a void of information and someone will fill it.

Some questions are inevitable: How's the company doing? What are the plans and how will they affect me? Why are we making changes?

It's naïve to think that our employees will simply shrug, consider it none of their business, and go on with their work. When we don't answer their questions, they find answers. And in most cases their answers are not the ones we'd prefer, often much worse than the truth. Unlikely possibilities grow into perceived realities, creating negative feelings and distrust of the company.

Sharing the truth is almost always better than risking the stories that inevitably spread.

Writing promotes understanding —and misunderstanding.

Writing is an excellent way to provide instructions, tie down processes, and record agreements. Written documents can be precise and are perfect for facts because they don't drift and fade like our memories do.

But writing is also a dangerous way to convey information since it's subject to misinterpretation of our feelings and intentions. Phrases that we mean to be helpful, supportive, and encouraging can be read as condescending, impatient, facetious, or disrespectful, backfiring to an effect opposite of that intended.

In sensitive situations it's usually best to meet face-to-face, where body language, facial expression, vocal inflection, and interactive conversation help convey our true meaning. When that's not possible, a phone call has at least the advantages of vocal inflection and interactive conversation.

The boss's words have exponential powers.

Employees remember things the boss says long after he's forgotten them. They replay the phrases in their minds, analyze them, interpret them multiple ways, bend them into meanings he never intended, take them home for second opinions, and lie awake agonizing over them. (This, no doubt, is the reason many managers become more reserved and less talkative than those they work with.)

With such added weight to our communications, there's little need to add emphasis or "pound the message home." Our people are listening carefully and give our suggestions serious consideration—even when they don't seem to.

> "A boss's mere expression of an opinion can be interpreted as a decision—even a direct order—by a staff member caught in the clutches of risk avoidance."
>
> —R. Alec MacKenzie

284

Employees don't quit their jobs; they quit their managers.

A poor relationship with the manager is the impetus for leaving a job more often than working conditions, pay, better opportunity, or any of the other often cited reasons, regardless of what the employee says.

In most cases the cause for quitting is a confrontation that indicates a lack of respect for the employee, his work, or his motives. A manager's short burst of anger or frustration leaves lasting scars.

Most employees would rather find other work than risk continuing conflict—even when they otherwise enjoy the job.

PEOPLE PROBLEMS

285

***We can expect perfection in others
when we find it in the mirror.***

There are no perfect employees. Some aspect of everyone can stand improvement—organization, focus, punctuality, sociability, accuracy, patience, determination, appearance, manners, language, etc. Life has too many facets for any of us to be ideal in all of them.

Replacing an employee for a minor shortcoming is seldom an effective remedy. We only trade faults we know for others we don't; the range is wide and some are much more than minor aggravations.

Our task is not collecting perfect people, but collecting good people whose strengths in their particular jobs outweigh their weaknesses.

Two pieces of praise
make criticism a palatable sandwich.

Suggestions for improvement needn't be as sensitive as some fear. Establishing a regular routine of discussing progress is key, and balancing suggestions with compliments keeps the conversation positive. "Nice job on .... How do you think you're doing with ...? I noticed you've gotten really good at .... To solve your challenge with ..., have you considered ...? Congratulations on ...."

A manager's role is combination coach/cheerleader/ fan. Once employees recognize that, channels of communication can open wide.

There's never a need
to remind them who's boss.

Despite the cliché, no employee ever really forgets who's the boss. A manager's authority looms constantly over the workplace and all employees fear his disapproval.

A manager who reminds employees of his authority, directly, by insinuation, or even in subtle body language, is resented. No one likes being at someone else's mercy. And the implications of imposing authority— that an employee must be commanded to do what's right—are an insult likely to do lasting damage to motivation and attitudes.

The philosophy that employees want to do what's right because it's right, not because we tell them to, is quickly recognized and subscribed to. If someone on staff doesn't fit this description, they simply don't belong in the company.

We gain respect and appreciation when we treat employees as collaborators and are reluctant to wield our authority.

The measure of a manager is the situations he can handle amiably.

Getting things done is the basic requirement of management; getting things done willingly and enthusiastically is the high art of management. The difference is significant—it determines how much and how well work is done, as well as the quality and longevity of employees.

Impatience and frustration are in the definition of manager, but they should never show a public face. A good manager can deliver even the most difficult messages with respect and consideration.

Assume you lack sufficient context to understand disappointing results.

Employees are seldom as dumb, unmotivated, or selfish as poor outcomes make them seem. In most cases their decisions and actions are not that different than ours would be given the same circumstances.

It can be an expensive mistake to summarily attribute fault for any situation without first asking for information. Many times what seemed like a poor decision, inadequate effort, or even insubordination turns out to be a valiant effort in difficult circumstances. If we rush to conclusions, employees rarely forget our misjudgment of their character. An apology in no way makes up.

Everyone deserves an opportunity to explain themselves.

Mistakes seldom need our interpretation.

Errors are easy to see after the fact—hindsight doesn't require genius.

In most cases an employee who has made a mistake knows exactly what went wrong and how to avoid it next time. Such situations don't need much from the manager. Constructive review is occasionally helpful; preaching, ranting and scolding are counterproductive.

Understanding and reassurance are often a surprising response that builds confidence and motivation (as well as appreciation).

When an employee can't do the work, the fault is often our own.

Inadequate performance is usually not an intentional offense. Often it's caused by a lack of information or training, misunderstanding of goals, or temporary difficulty in grasping a critical job skill. In these cases we have an obligation to help the employee become a more valuable team member.

Even if the problem is more deep-seated—a personality mismatch for the job, inadequate educational or cultural background, lack of an innate skill—we have some responsibility for our error in hiring, especially if the employee left another job to take this one.

If the employee simply can't do the work with reasonable coaching and training, sometimes we can find him another job in the company more suited to his skills and abilities. (However moving him where inadequate performance won't be as noticeable is never a valid solution.) If not, we can offer reasonable severance, a letter of reference citing his desirable attributes (everyone has some), and sometimes help in finding a more appropriate job.

A poor performance appraisal should never be a surprise.

Employees need and deserve to know how they're doing. Regular feedback encourages good employees to even better performance, and gives inadequate employees the opportunity to improve or look for more suitable work.

A poor appraisal shouldn't be confrontational or offensive. When we begin by asking for their own assessment, they usually sum it up pretty accurately and we need only agree. If they miss an important aspect, we should ask about it. In the rare case they're totally off, we have to give a contrary opinion, but it seldom requires heavy emphasis; their hearing on this topic is acute. It's a simple and friendly discussion, and with continuous communication none of it should come as a surprise.

When asked what they would like to do, they'll almost always say they'd like to try to do better and usually can offer a plan. If it seems feasible, we should welcome their effort and tell them we're pulling for them.

A person without drive can't be driven.

Drive, determination, and persistence come from deep within the personality. If they're not there, we can't put them there. We can push unmotivated employees into short term performance but, despite their best efforts, they soon get tired and fall back into their old habits.

Both employee and company are better off if the employee finds another job that doesn't require initiative and self-motivation. (Yes, there are some—just not in retailing.)

Listen, think;
think, speak.

Quick answers can create long and difficult problems. As much as we might like to, we just can't reel words back in and start again. And the worse the gaffe, the more memorable and lasting it is.

We don't have to have ready answers to every problem. When we're faced with a new or unusual question or issue, we can almost always afford a little time to think before responding. "Let me get back to you on that," or "Let's make a time to talk about it," aren't admissions of inadequacy; they're acknowledgements that we take the issue seriously and value an intelligent answer.

I once worked with an attorney who pondered his fingertips seemingly for eternity whenever I posed a complex question. The first few times I wondered if he was summoning up anger-control or reliving college recreational experiences. But I soon got used to it and learned that his answers were accurate and thorough, often encompassing multiple scenarios. I developed a lot of trust in his opinions and would still be using him but, alas, he was appointed judge. Although the wait must be unbearable for defendants, I suspect few of his judgments are overturned.

Nothing is often a clever thing to say.

A raised eyebrow or faint frown is sometimes the only response we need give, especially to disappointing behavior. If our values are well known, our disapproval is often more powerful when we don't elaborate. Reviewing expectations is seldom necessary and "scolding" is demotivating.

The message is clear and there's little to add.

"I've never been hurt by anything I didn't say."

— Calvin Coolidge

The price of solution is thought.

People issues are always complicated by personalities and often have complex backgrounds. Typically we have a range of possible responses, each with its own set of side-effects. Choosing the best option often requires some thought, and considering the long-term implications, is usually worth the effort.

Putting thoughts on paper can help clarify them and make the solutions more obvious. Some relevant questions: What is the outcome I hope for? What options do I have? How would the person likely respond to each option? Which option is most likely to achieve the desired result? What is the best time and place to execute it?

We shouldn't take action until we can visualize and anticipate the outcome. "If we don't know where we're going, we might not like where we get."

> "When I'm getting ready to reason with a man, I spend one-third of my time thinking about myself and what I am going to say, and two-thirds thinking about him and what he is going to say."
>
> **—Abraham Lincoln**

Lose your temper,
lose your employee.

Offending or berating an employee serves no useful purpose and usually creates irreparable damage. In most cases the employee quits—if he doesn't walk out on the spot, he begins looking for another job, often leaving without notice when he finds it. He sometimes takes particular pleasure in leaving when his departure leaves us in a bind.

The old advice of "let your feelings out" or "get it off your chest" couldn't be more wrong. A few quick words in anger can destroy a relationship forever.

> "A man who cannot command his temper should not think of being a man of business."
>
> —**Lord Chesterfield**

Threats are the worst
of a manager's tools.

When an employee has so little buy-in to company goals that only a threat motivates him, he performs only when we're over his shoulder. In addition to being unreliable and unproductive, he frustrates motivated employees, serves as a bad example of what's acceptable, and drags down the attitudes and culture of the company.

Spare the threats and remove the cancer.

You don't have to be a detective to know who's not working.

We don't have to follow employees around, monitor arrival and departure times, view security videos, or snoop through phone records, documents, email, and Internet records to know who's wasting time. Either the employee is getting results or he's not.

For salespeople a printout of sales tells the story quickly and clearly. Others display a natural inclination to either stay on top of their work or coast along chronically behind.

The best management is clear communication of the results wanted and friendly joint review of the results produced.

The only appropriate "discipline" is de-hiring.

Discipline is for intentional screw-ups, not for mistakes. And since there's no place in our stores for employees who screw-up intentionally, the only "discipline" we need is our own in getting them out.

When an employee knowingly does something contrary to company goals, (repeatedly comes in late, fails to do necessary paperwork, discounts beyond policy, etc.), we can discuss the infraction (couched between recognition of the employee's good habits) and explain the problems it creates.

If the employee understands the objectives but isn't motivated enough to work toward them, discipline won't transform him into the employee we need; in most cases it will only worsen his motivation. The sooner we correct our hiring mistake the better.

My sister-in-law is a human relations manager in local government and we often discuss personnel challenges. When she asked what discipline procedures we have, she was surprised when I said, "None. We explain to them what we'd like. If that doesn't work, we let them go."

In government that would, of course, lead to extensive civil service appeals, lawsuits, reinstatements, back pay, etc.—which explains many government workers' attitudes and performance.

A manager is not a referee.

A manager can't resolve disputes between employees. Whatever solution he imposes will inevitably be resented by at least one side, and hard feelings not only remain but are ratcheted up by his involvement. The battle continues, only clandestinely, where damage runs deeper and is harder to resolve.

A dispute is over not when we say it is, but when the two parties decide they want to get along.

The solution is often in "asking" them to work it out: "It's not good for the company for the two of you to be fighting. Please get together and resolve this."

(Such a request includes implications that need no elaboration.)

People with the same information are of the same opinion.

Disagreements are seldom due to the selfishness and stupidity we sometimes attribute them to. In most cases they're the result of differing sets of information.

Each of us understands the challenges of our own jobs, but we're less aware of those of others. Accounting personnel know the problems caused by inaccurate invoicing, but they seldom experience the challenges and chaos of selling. Salespeople know the problems created by a botched delivery, but they rarely see the heroics demanded by some delivery conditions.

The solution to most disagreements is determining which information is not shared and making it available.

Our accounting people have to contend with many errors and omissions on our rental contracts. When contracts don't add up, they have to make the corrections and explain them to the customer. When a serial number isn't in the system or shows rented to another customer, they have to reach the customer and get the correct number. When addresses or phone numbers are missing or inaccurate, they have to do the detective work to fill them in. As can be expected, the salespeople are common topics of abuse.

Our rental business is highly seasonal (95 percent takes place in the few weeks after school opens), and in many cases one or two of our salespeople rent as many as 100 instruments in a one-hour meeting. As a result we sometimes call on accounting personnel to help salespeople at their meetings.

The impressions of the accounting people are reliable: "It's amazing they can handle so much so quickly and with so much going on." The experience buys the salespeople a few months of understanding.

The boss is always
too soft on everyone else.

Solutions to personnel problems are obvious to everyone who has never managed: Reprimand and punish the offender—the more severely, the less likely the offense is to recur.

If we ask how they would feel if we treated them that way, their response is dependable: "Fine, because I'd know I deserved it. But, of course, I'd never do that."

Maybe not, but everyone makes a mistake or shows a fault sooner or later. And their response to the treatment they advocate would more likely be: "Why the hell is he coming down on me?! Doesn't he know how hard I work for this company?! This guy's a real bastard! Why should I stay with a company that doesn't appreciate me?!"

Patience, understanding, and respect are always appropriate—regardless of the helpful advice of employees.

The risk of lending to an employee
isn't the money but the employee.

An employee's request for a loan or advance is hard to resist. It almost always involves a pressing need and it would be a cold employer who doesn't care about his people.

But the employee's appreciation for the loan is soon more than offset by the need to repay it, and our willingness to help leads to exactly the opposite effect we intended.

Financial problems are rarely solved in a week or a month; bills and living expenses continue, and are only compounded by additional debt. An employee who can't repay what he's borrowed imagines hard feelings and dreads a confrontation, even if we never give the debt another thought. A loyal and enthusiastic attitude turns into defensiveness and rationalization.

Agreed-upon payroll deductions reduce the potential for repayment conflict. But they also reduce pay, the main incentive for working, sometimes enough that low-level employees stop coming.

Finding an opportunity for the employee to earn some extra money that doesn't have to be repaid is often a better solution. When that's not possible, a gift often yields better results than a loan.

FIRING

305

A business is the sum of the performance of its people.

A store can excel only when its people perform excellently. If we tolerate incompetence, nonperformance, or apathy in our employees, nothing else can make up; the handicap is simply too great to overcome.

Good employees are often tempted to leave for better jobs, while poor employees are grateful to stay where they are. If we're passive and accept these tendencies as chronic and inevitable conditions of retail, our stores are eventually staffed only by poor employees.

A well-run retail store is never created passively; in every case someone is relentless in pursuing high standards—and that includes, specifically and especially, shedding employees whose work doesn't meet the standards.

We owe it to our employees
not to tolerate poor performance.

It's frustrating and demoralizing to good employees when someone around them can't or won't do his job. If they have no power to change or replace him, their choice is either to adjust their standards downward or find another job. As a result a few incompetents or bad attitudes can have a devastating effect on a company.

Our employees know who isn't doing his job. They're waiting for signals from us whether such performance is acceptable. Almost all hope it's not. And because non-performers make less effort to conceal their inadequacies from their co-workers than from their boss, co-workers typically wonder why we wait so long.

People don't change;
we have to change people.

It's tempting to believe an employee with bad habits can be coached and improved. Sometimes the needed change seems so logical, simple and important that it's hard to imagine the offender wouldn't understand and cooperate. And if an appeal to his logic fails, surely restructured compensation or threats and discipline will get through.

But such efforts typically yield little more than frustration and wasted time. They will occasionally cause a person to attempt changes, but the changes are virtually always short-lived.

Most habits and attitudes are no longer daily choices; they're deeply imbedded in the personality. Personalities are like tempered steel; with enough pressure they can be bent temporarily, but as soon as the pressure is released they return to their natural states.

> Whenever I'm tempted to try to change an employee, I remind myself how much trouble I have changing myself.

Low turnover is a problem too.

Occasionally we hear a business manager brag that he doesn't lose employees. While that probably does indicate an attractive work environment, it doesn't mean everyone on the staff deserves to be there.

A good job attracts and retains both good and bad employees. No manager has a perfect hiring record; all need to correct their mistakes and remove employees who don't belong.

> Long-time GE CEO Jack Welch required managers to eliminate the bottom ten percent of employees each year. He reasoned that it was good not only for the organization but for the individuals because it took them out of situations in which they were failing.

An employee who tries but can't deserves a different job.

Occasionally an employee has a good attitude, wants to contribute, puts in sufficient time and effort, but simply can't get the desired results. We could fire him but that seems cruel, perhaps even unfair since he's done everything we've asked. And, after all, we made the hiring mistake.

When good attitude and effort don't bring satisfactory results, the employee is in the wrong job—his personality and aptitudes are different than those required.

Motivation and drive are valuable, and can almost always be profitably employed. If we can find or create another job that better matches his personality and skills, he can often be turned into a loyal and profitable long-term employee.

If a better match for his abilities can't be found within the company, perhaps we can help him find something more suitable outside.

310

Moving an unmotivated employee to an out-of-the-way job only enables worse performance.

Putting a poor employee into a less important job is often a tempting alternative to firing him. We rationalize that his inadequacies will be less critical there and less costly to the company.

But an employee without motivation performs even worse where his performance isn't noticed. Such plans don't solve the problem—they hide and aggravate it.

The only proper solution for lack of motivation is to get it out of the company. Firing is unpleasant but it's a bargain compared to living long term with poor performance. There is no place in a good business for a person who doesn't share and eagerly contribute to its goals.

311

An employee who requires constant supervision is seldom worth employing.

Most employees are eager to participate and play a valuable role in the company. With training and an understanding of what's to be accomplished, they gladly do their part, requiring only occasional assistance and guidance.

Others however are immature or have deep emotional problems and will not perform adequately on their own. These people are almost unemployable since constant supervision seldom makes economic sense, especially for their minimally acceptable efforts.

> "Never try to work a man who will work you to death trying to work him."
>
> —Robert Lewis Wilson

Loyalty and longevity deserve support and understanding.

Almost everyone, at some point in life, experiences personal or family problems—divorce, serious illness, accidents, troubled children, loss of family members, etc. When our long-term employees run into these, they deserve consideration beyond economics. They are our company's family and we can't abandon them in their time of need.

If a long-term employee can no longer do his job, we can usually turn up some possibilities—revising his responsibilities, moving him to another job, creating a job more compatible to his skills.—there is almost always some opportunity for him to earn his keep.

If there really is nothing for him, we can help him find another suitable job and support him in the transition.

313

An employee who knows how he's doing doesn't have to be fired.

Helping employees recognize when their performance is inadequate avoids the unpleasantness, hard feelings, embarrassment, and legal complications of firing. Regular communication inspires those who are doing well to even better performance and encourages those who are sub-par to either improve or move on to work that better suits them.

We can initiate a candid conversation with an underperforming employee simply by asking how he thinks he's doing. In most cases his own assessment will be pretty close; when it's not, we have to clarify the expectations he has somehow missed.

In some cases he'll make the adjustments, but often he just can't change long term. After a few friendly consultations, he'll almost always find something else to do. No one wants to stay where they aren't respected and appreciated as team members.

The process is much less painful than firing. There's no public embarrassment, no detrimental record, no co-worker resentment, and usually no long-term hard feelings.

314

When dismissal is ominous, it often comes as a relief.

An employee who is doing poorly almost always knows it. He feels the pressure and is uncomfortable in the job.

In most cases he recognizes what has to happen, and, if he doesn't do it himself, fears only how it will be handled. When it's done professionally, discreetly, and with empathy, he's usually relieved and sometimes even thankful.

No paycheck is adequate compensation for misery at work. In the long run he's better off in a job he does well and takes pride in.

There is a job to match almost every skill set, and pride, satisfaction, and appreciation are the rewards that go to those who find it.

315

Personnel changes can fit the business schedule.

Dismissing an employee impulsively is messy and expensive—someone must cover his position, handle his duties, finish his transactions, follow through on his promises, etc. Not having someone available for these things, not realizing which things need to be done, or not knowing how to do them can be costly.

Most personnel changes can be planned to fit the company's schedule. The best time might be between projects, after we've collected needed information, after a big sale is completed, after we've hired a replacement, when the replacement is trained, after an upcoming event, when vacations are over, or after the busy season.

Firing should be polite, firm, and quick.

Firing doesn't require a long explanation, nor does a debate of the reasons and their merit serve any useful purpose. It should be simple, blameless, and respectful.

The best time is usually at the end of a workday when everyone else is leaving. In a quiet, private place simply tell the employee it didn't work out. Extend to him whatever severance is appropriate. Then help him gather his things, walk him to the door, and wish him luck.

No further conversation is necessary. (With some exceptions by state and contract, most employment is considered "at-will"—either employer or employee may legally terminate employment whenever they like, with or without reason.)

317

Terminations must be immediate.

There's good reason for firing a poor employee late on Friday afternoon and walking him to the door. Allowing an employee to work the rest of a day or any other period after we've told him he's being terminated just doesn't work. The situation attracts attention, arouses sympathy, and stirs up hard feelings. In addition a fired employee isn't likely to get much work done, and might even attempt to sabotage the company.

Nor does it work to offer him the option to resign with notice. He won't be able to contain his feelings and will share with his co-workers all the usual rationalizations—the boss just doesn't like me or plays favorites, the job is too big for one person, management doesn't understand the difficulty of the job, directions were unclear or conflicting, got no cooperation, etc. Regardless of his reputation for non-performance, his situation will attract sympathy and generate hard feelings.

A secrecy agreement is counterproductive since it typically restricts only us—he'll simply precede his story with an admonition not to let us know he told them. All the information available will then be one-sided and emotionally biased, and no one will be able to talk about it openly.

318

Accounting isn't just a tax project.

For many small businesses accounting is the dreaded annual chore of determining the taxman's bite. And until the accountant finishes (and we adjust the results to better suit our tastes and budgets), the outcome is more suspenseful than a John Grisham adventure.

Income tax might be the most required of accounting's uses, but it is by no means the most important. Accounting is supposed to serve four parties—management, ownership, creditors, and the tax collector—and they belong in that order. Only when the first does its job will the other three be happy.

Accounting is management's map. Would we drive a whole year before we look where we're going? Yogi was right: "If we don't know where we're going, we might end up someplace else."

"Gut feel" is an illusion; numbers are reality.

Sometimes we can sense a trend. We feel busier, expenses seem higher (never lower), traffic looks thin or brisk, a product appears to sell well or poorly, competitors seem more visible and aggressive, a salesperson looks busier, negotiating seems more prevalent, etc.

Such a sense is one of the rewards of experience; detecting a problem or opportunity is the first step in fixing or exploiting it.

But before we set changes in motion we do well to confirm our hunches, since the numbers occasionally prove us wrong. Most shifts are too subtle or complex to feel, and the difference between profit and loss is almost always too narrow to sense without exact numbers. Trends become clear only when we make them numeric.

When we have the numbers, we know where we are and where we're headed. The path is illuminated and we can proceed with confidence.

Management without numbers assumes the worst.

A manager has to consider and be prepared for all the possibilities. Unfortunately the most impressionable are the major problems, including, especially, losses and financial shortfalls.

We can handle most other situations so there's no need to dwell on them. But what would we do if income doesn't cover expenses? Or cash in the bank isn't enough to pay the bills? Anyone who hasn't lost sleep to those questions isn't a retailer; it's the profession's price of admission.

We can relieve ourselves of most fears simply by figuring out where we are. As numbers clarify the picture, some of the possibilities are eliminated. We might find we haven't struck the vein we set out for, but it's consoling to at least know we'll be able to continue the search.

Even when the predicament proves troubling, understanding it has a calming effect. Much psychology can be summarized by, "If I knew what I was so worried about, I wouldn't be so worried."

Daily results might surprise, but monthly and annual should never.

Month and year-end statements are only summaries of activity and trends we should be tracking continuously throughout the month and year.

Business activity should be posted as it happens. Ideally no entry, audit, or correction needs to wait for month-end.

There's no reason to wonder how we're doing when we can press the button and see it now, in time to make adjustments.

Accounting quality is set at the top.

Good accounting is by no means an automatic function in retail. We get it only when we commit resources (knowledgeable people, up-to-date equipment, quality software, etc.), establish well-designed systems, and insist on timeliness and accuracy.

Physics' Law of Entropy applies in accounting also: "A system, when left to itself, tends to a state of maximum disorder." If we tolerate inaccurate numbers, meaningless reports, and late financial statements, they quickly devolve into new standards. As fewer people find the information credible and useful, accounting deteriorates toward irrelevance. Eventually staff performs the routines without anyone understanding or asking why.

Accurate and timely accounting occurs only to the degree that management appreciates its value, is committed to and insists on its production, and champions its cause.

Year-end corrections render the whole year's statements worthless and deceptive.

Significant adjustments made at or after year-end mean all the preceding statements were not only wrong but deceiving. They mislead us in our decisions and cause us and all of our people to lose confidence in our accounting.

All the numbers on financial statements need to be checked and confirmed regularly, and discrepancies resolved immediately as discovered. Inventories should be counted and adjusted in continuous cycles, receivables examined and tested on a regular schedule, payables verified, and every entry on the balance sheet and income statement compared to reports and physical checks. Even the balance sheet itself must be confirmed, since, despite its name, it doesn't always balance.

Year-end should be no more than a cut-off date, and final results shouldn't differ significantly from those the staff has been tracking until the close of the last day's business.

Chronically-behind is a symptom of personality, not overload.

We sometimes become so accustomed to backlogs that we believe they're unavoidable conditions of the environment. "There's just so much work to do that we stay two weeks behind."

The truth is that many people stay behind regardless of their load. Their work expands to fill their time, and until they've reached the limit of acceptable delay they see no reason to hurry.

Ultimately the amount of work is the same whether done today or two weeks from now. If the backlog were suddenly gone, we could keep up with the work coming in—no additional staff needed. And in most cases staying current is less work since it avoids the innate confusion and inefficiencies of being behind.

If work is falling further behind, more staff might be needed. If work is being done but chronically late, what's needed is a shift in expectations.

Financial statements should be defined by the business, not by the software.

Standard software financial statements might satisfy bankers and accountants, but they just don't fit the needs of retailers. They have stiff or fixed formats, apply percentages in the wrong places and to the wrong numbers, don't allow complex allocations of expenses by departments, locations, and activities, don't create the most useful ratios, give incomplete department and location net profits, and allow little adaptation or customization.

Relying on these statements exclusively for financial information is like looking through a periscope—the view may be OK in the open ocean, but it's far too restricted to steer around obstacles and through complex traffic.

Ideal statements are feasible only when we ignore feasibility.

We have to forget the limitations of our software and sketch out our ideal statement—categorize and departmentalize income and expenses, allocate expenses where they're actually incurred, calculate percentages wherever they're pertinent, create every ratio and indicator we consider useful, and compute department and location income and expense all the way to net profit.

Once we establish how we want the statements, we can figure out how to create them. Rarely can it be done within standard accounting software. Usually the numbers must be exported to spreadsheets where we can arrange them in the order and format we need.

Design and setup requires thought and time, but maintenance can be quick and easy. Spreadsheet software can automatically retrieve updated numbers each month and calculate the statements.

Just because it's legal
doesn't mean it's accurate.

Accounting conventions like LIFO, accelerated depreciation, and lower of cost and value are tax gifts and accountants' CYAs, not attempts at correct valuations.

Tax law is full of economic incentives and political pork; GAAP is weighted down with accountants' conservatism. Together they make it difficult for us or anyone else to get an accurate picture of our companies.

Accountants will argue that their numbers are absolutely correct—they can show us the specific tax laws and GAAP proclamations to prove it. Actual economic value isn't part of their logic. If we insist on a more accurate picture, they might grant us a footnote on their statement to make our case.

Let the accountants create their tax and GAAP fantasies and tell us what we owe. Meanwhile to run our businesses we have to create statements that show us in no-BS hard numbers where we are and how we're doing.

Accounting inaccuracies are reprieves from responsibility.

When we rational humans are faced with news that doesn't suit us, we often put our talents and faculties to work denying it. In business, financial results are too often the target of our rationalization.

If we don't like our results and an inaccuracy is handy, we and our managers cling to it as evidence that the ultimate conclusions are wrong. Even when the error is small and relatively inconsequential, we reason that it's representative of more and bigger problems in the data.

Unless our accounting is above reproach, we can interpret it however we like. Poor results become tolerable, the status quo acceptable, problems benign, and no one is disturbed from his comfort zone.

On the other hand, when the numbers are beyond reproach, our thoughts turn from rationalization to strategy. We focus on improving the business.

> "So convenient a thing it is to be a reasonable creature, since it enables one to find or make a reason for everything one has a mind to do."
>
> **—Ben Franklin**

Manage the business, not the numbers.

There's latitude in every financial statement—depreciation can be immediate, accelerated, or stretched, appreciated or depreciated asset values can be recognized or deferred, bad debts and shrinkage written off or maintained, expenses pulled forward or pushed back .... Even the most rigid interpretation of accounting rules leaves wiggle room for those who prefer biased results.

When we focus on bending the numbers, we waste valuable effort that should be spent managing the business. Better to face the music and fix the business, not the numbers.

Wishful accounting is a tangled web.

Creativity is a wonderful asset—but not in accounting.

When financial statements are stretched to suit one of their four masters—management, owners, creditors, and the tax man—there's a cost to pay to the other three.

Underreporting income to hold taxes down deflates the results creditors want to see. Overstating income to satisfy owners and creditors increases tax liability, sometimes when the company can least afford it. And all inaccurate numbers make it difficult for management to interpret the real condition of the company and establish accountability.

Fictitious accounting is a loan shark with a crushing interest rate.

Bending numbers is only a temporary reprieve; sooner or later the piper must be paid.

Bogus numbers carry over on the balance sheet from year to year and build with each creative entry. They make correction of both the numbers and the business' underlying problems an even more daunting challenge.

Poor results are usually concealed in inflated inventory, worthless receivables, and unrecognized payables. Each year of compounding makes them stick out more. When they can no longer be hidden, their correction is likely to make sane bankers and creditors run for the exits.

Fictions that understate results (to save taxes) are usually hidden in unrecognized inventory and receivables. Once stashed, they stay there, occasionally for rainy-day income smoothing, but most often until detected in a tax audit when penalties and interest are slapped on.

Better to take our lumps as we earn them, work on the business instead of the numbers, and sleep soundly.

Manipulations are the last entries of the year—as every auditor knows.

It's usually fairly simple to see whether financial results have been manipulated and which way simply by examining the last few ledger entries of the year. In most cases the adjustments are made weeks or months after the end of the fiscal year and are changes to the value of receivables or inventory.

Once the auditor can see the placement and direction of the bias, auditing the particular asset or liability turns up the amount of discrepancy.

Shrinkage and bad debts are continuous and should be recognized that way.

Annual adjustments for shrinkage and bad debts are typically the deadly big surprises at the end of the year. They often change the bottom line significantly, rendering all preceding statements useless and misleading.

There's no reason to wait for the end of the year. When inventory is counted on a cycle schedule, shrinkage is recognized continuously throughout the year. Reviewing receivables monthly and writing off doubtful accounts according to fixed criteria accrues the effects gradually and reveals their trends.

There's no year-end rush, no anxiety about "how we really did," and no surprises. Everyone sees the numbers as they develop, before it's too late to do anything about them.

Take shrinkage before investigating; reverse shrinkage if you find it.

When we discover merchandise is missing it's just not in our nature to summarily write it off. Taking it to shrinkage implies resignation and acceptance that it's gone, probably stolen, and that offends our principles. We have a moral and financial obligation to resist theft, so we resolve to investigate. Until the crime is solved and the merchandise is found, the investigation remains open—and our inventory records are never adjusted.

Better to recognize shrinkage as soon as it's detected and add it back later if we locate the merchandise. Taking the shrinkage doesn't impede the investigation; in most cases it creates a more convenient list of items to search for.

(In some stores there is considerable movement and flux in inventory. As a result many items that are missing in one count turn up in the next. In these cases it's often more efficient to count often and establish a shrinkage rule, such as items that are missing three consecutive cycle counts are shrunk.)

Auditing isn't just for auditors.

Auditing ourselves regularly uncovers small problems before they turn into big ones and prevents unpleasant surprises at year-end.

Audits should be on a rotating schedule and can be performed by the controller or accounting personnel. It doesn't have to be a complete check and count of all inventory, receivables, assets and liabilities. A sampling as small as 1-2 percent of each area is usually representative and uncovers underlying problems.

The auditor should make no attempt to fix the problems, only to report on them. Responsibility for correcting all records (not just the sample) and keeping them accurate stays with the area manager.

Employees need financial statements too.

There is no feedback, challenge, or recognition more effective than a financial statement. It allows managers and staff to see and understand goals, focus efforts, track progress, and share in the pride and disappointment of results.

We have to get over our concerns that employees can't handle profit information. Hopefully we haven't hired anyone so naïve as to not realize that a store must make a profit. Better to acknowledge margins and expenses than to let employees assume gross margins (which they would inevitably discover anyway) simply go into the owners' pockets. Profit is easily explained as necessary not only to cover salaries and expenses, but for the store to grow, buy more inventory, replace fixtures and equipment, etc.

Staff can see daily revenue and expense opportunities that management doesn't notice. When they have a clear picture of the objectives and challenges, they can influence results. As a company grows and management functions are dispersed, financial statements provide the ideal feedback and performance appraisal.

Over the years our department and location financial statements have evolved into one-page condensations detailing all of the area's income and expenses all the way to a bottom-line profit or loss. They include inventories, margin percentages, inventory and advertising budgets, previous years' numbers, ratios, and goals—a condensed summary of all numbers relevant to the area's performance.

Employees look forward to their distribution on the eighth of each month and celebrate or lament the outcomes; the best results are recognized at our weekly company meetings.

We encourage each manager to sit down with the controller to discuss (and argue) allocations and get explanations for every number that looks unlikely or that they don't understand.

CASH FLOW

337

Profit isn't cash flow and is often its opposite.

At some point every successful retailer asks, "If I'm doing so well, where the hell's the money?"

One of the great disappointments of retailing is that making a profit doesn't mean having cash in the bank. Profits require sales, and sales require investments in inventory, leasehold improvements, and equipment. The problem is compounded further when sales go to accounts receivable.

Profits do improve the balance sheet but the enhancement is rarely to cash in the bank.

Ironically, it's only when the cycle slows and investment is reduced that cash becomes available.

After ten years of double-digit sales growth, I was depressed to find that our debt had increased with every sales increase. The company was profitable and equity was growing, but we couldn't take it out and it appeared we never would—it was becoming more difficult to get even our salaries out. It seemed our success wasn't making us wealthy; it was getting us deeper into debt. And transferring company ownership to the next generation, a seemingly unending process in our family business, was getting ever more complex.

Our projections showed we simply couldn't continue the sales increases indefinitely—we didn't have the resources to support them. The exercise forced us to plan slower growth, cut out non-productive investments, work on improved efficiency, and hold leverage within acceptable bounds.

That realization, as disconcerting as it was, probably saved us from ourselves.

You can go broke making a profit.

Profit is the revered (and maligned) objective of business—the elusive reward for hard work and services well-performed, as well as the ultimate score in the competition to meet customers' needs. An experienced retailer rarely forgets his profit focus.

But profit doesn't pay the bills—cash does. Until profit becomes liquid, it does nothing to meet our obligations to the landlord, the utility company, our suppliers, and our employees, not to mention our families.

Turning away profit is not in the character of a business person. Yet, if enough of that profit gets stuck in inventory, receivables, equipment, facilities, or any of the other myriad investments of retail, we can't pay our bills.

Bankruptcy doesn't mean unprofitable—it means not enough cash to meet obligations.

Profit is often an illusion; cash flow is fact.

There's a lot of play in an income statement; even within the rules of accounting, a creative businessman or accountant can make it say almost anything he wants, at least for a while.

Cash isn't so nebulous. It's either in the bank or it isn't. The business can either pay its bills or it can't. Investors can either be repaid or more investment must be sought.

With profit-and-loss you can change the tune; with cash flow you have to face the music.

Taking a loss is only a sickness;
running out of cash is the fatality.

Losses are depressing; nobody likes to go backward. We resent the effort and investment that not only didn't produce rewards but depleted equity.

But losses don't force us out of business; running out of cash does.

A business with cash has the luxury of time. It can think through its plans and strategies, make adjustments, experiment, wait out downturns, invest against the cycles, build to meet long-term projections, and even bet against the odds.

As long as cash is available, the business can continue—regardless of profit or loss.

Cash flow is a surprise
only when you're not looking.

Overdue payments to vendors, buying freezes, missed payrolls, and panicked calls to bankers are some stores' normal business routines. In most cases these "emergencies" are due not to unforeseeable business results but simply failure to project cash. Sometimes management doesn't know how, but often it just doesn't go to the trouble.

Barring wild and unpredictable swings in business, there really is little excuse for not anticipating cash. The numbers are almost always available and the calculations aren't difficult.

Only an accountant could love an accountant's cash flow statement.

The cash flow statements prepared by accountants are the most awkward and consequently the least useful of standard financial statements.

Few CEOs say they use the traditional cash flow statement for business planning; source and application is just not a format most think and work in.

As sure as the balance sheet balances, cash is what's left when we project the rest.

Financial statements are equations: sales and other income minus cost-of-goods and expenses equal net profit; assets equal liabilities plus equity and net profit. As a result, if we know all the numbers on the income and balance sheets but one, we can calculate it. (If it doesn't work, it's time for a new accountant.)

Using this math it's fairly easy to create a spreadsheet in the income statement and balance sheet format and have it calculate backwards to cash.

To project monthly cash for a year, set up 13 columns—beginning of the year balances plus each month's results. Estimate monthly sales, gross margins, and expenses; each month's resulting profit adds to equity on the balance sheet and carries over to the next month. Then estimate monthly levels for inventories, receivables, payables, and loans. With all the other numbers filled in, the spreadsheet can calculate how much cash will be in the bank each month.

If one month's projection shows too little or too much cash in the bank, make the adjustments you prefer—increase or decrease the bank loan, raise or lower inventories, pay down payables, etc. After each change, the spreadsheet adjusts cash in the bank.

As the year progresses replace the projected numbers with actual results. (Italics can indicate projections while a normal font indicates actual results.) The updates automatically make changes in the remaining projected cash figures, keeping you aware of developing problems and allowing you to make the needed changes before they become crises.

A cash flow projection is a feasibility study.

No significant project, investment, or financial plan can be wise without consideration of its effects on cash.

Expansions, new ventures, added locations, staff additions, etc., often have exciting potential for profit, but their allure is a dangerous trap if the company can't afford their cash flow implications.

A cash flow projection calculates how much of an opportunity a store can afford, how and how long a company can endure a downturn or a competitive threat, when and how much creditors and investors can be repaid, and when owners can (finally) take out some accumulated profit.

Cash return, not profit, is the measure of an investment.

An investor, whether individual or business, can't spend profit; an investment's value is realized only if and when profit becomes cash.

A business investment that promises high profit has little value if the profit remains stuck in inventory, receivables, equipment, or any of the other necessities of business.

The appeal of profit lies in its potential to be turned into cash. Then and only then does it take on true value to the business and its owners.

Growth doesn't produce cash, it consumes it.

Retailers love growth. When we ask, "How's business?" we mean, "Are sales up or down?" Up a little is good; up a lot is better. Like gluttons and addicts, we crave all the sales we can get. Turning sales away is irrefutable evidence of retail insanity.

Ironically we'd be in deep trouble if we got all the sales we wanted—helpless victims of compulsive suicide.

Retail growth is expensive. Additional inventory must be purchased, sales and office facilities expanded, fixtures added, leasehold improvements made, employees hired and trained, receivables expanded ....

Cash rarely flows in with retail growth—it flows out. Added sales seldom repay their investments quickly; growing is a long-term investment. Meanwhile leverage creeps up, making the expanding retailer increasingly vulnerable.

More than a few profitable retailers have been victims of their own success, growing themselves into financial trouble and occasionally even extinction.

Not all businesses suffer the same cash challenges as most retailers. A friend in the school fundraising business deals in magazine subscriptions. Students collect orders and payments from relatives, friends, and neighbors. My friend submits the subscriptions to the magazine publishers and is billed later. As a result his bank account often swells to hundreds of thousands—the higher his sales, the greater his cash.

Perhaps if manufacturers would bill retailers only after the merchandise is sold and the money collected...

When sales go down cash often goes up.

Just as increasing sales requires increasing investment, decreasing sales allows decreasing investment. Some sold inventory doesn't have to be replaced, less is tied up in receivables, equipment doesn't have to be replaced as often, etc.

As a result, downturns need not be catastrophes. When expenses are kept in line with sales, downturns are simply breathers or resizing, with the major consolation that cash is freed. Debts can be paid, leverage reduced, and accumulated equity distributed.

We've often been amazed at how long a declining competitor can hang on. While they're clearly losing sales and customers, manufacturers are deserting them, and their systems and facilities are growing more antiquated by the day, they keep going as if nothing has changed.

The business-down/cash-up effect explains how they can endure such long declines. Despite continuous losses eating away at their equity, every step downward frees cash.

As long as the owner is able to ignore or rationalize the equity deterioration, he can ride the trend slowly and gently to the bottom.

348

Bankers aren't venture capitalists.

Many businesspeople would say bankers have thoroughly earned their conservative reputations—they make loans only when repayment is guaranteed in every way they can conjure. Even when secured assets are more than sufficient to assure loan recovery, they like to have our homes, cars, investments, and future earnings on the line, too.

Bankers are quick to point out that their rates are cheaper than other sources because they reflect this minimized risk. Fair enough—the interest we pay a bank doesn't include much premium to cover loan losses.

When our funding needs can't be guaranteed with assets or other worth, bankers probably aren't the right source. Partners, stockholders, or venture capitalists are more likely bets.

349

Bankers want you most when you need them least.

According to Mark Twain, "A banker is a fellow who lends you his umbrella when the sun is shining and wants it back the minute it begins to rain."

We have to make a convincing case that the sun is shining, we can easily pay back, with interest, what we propose to borrow, and that we have financing alternatives. Confidence and an air of independence (along with a realistic plan) go a long way.

We don't tell a banker we "need a loan;" we say we're "considering our financing options." We don't say another bank turned our loan down; we say we're "talking to other banks, too." And we don't say we need a new banking relationship; we say we've already got a bank "but it never hurts to talk."

350

Bankers want loans other bankers want.

Assessing the worthiness of a loan is as subjective as choosing a mate—what one finds attractive is sometimes inexplicable to others. But when everyone else seems enthralled, popular judgment reassures us and we'd consider ourselves fortunate to be chosen from among so many.

Repayment risks aren't easily determined and bankers have considerable latitude in filling their loan portfolios. While almost all subscribe to various sets of formulas, most don't allow them to deter loans they want to make. Sometimes the ultimate validation of a loan is the fact that other bankers are pursuing it, too.

> In the '80s relentless self-promoter Donald Trump had the world's top banks standing in line to lend to him. By their own admissions many "adjusted their own risk/reward ratios," ignored accepted lending requirements, and eagerly loaned him more than the costs of his projects.
>
> Not one to miss an opportunity to boast or to profit, Trump touted his technique in his books: Make the banks believe you have lots of financing options and you don't need them.
>
> The technique was undeniably effective, allowing him to accrue over $9 billion in debt— unfortunately more than the Donald could repay.

The loan committee is a classroom, your banker the student, and your application the lesson.

For all but the smallest of loans, convincing a banker we're creditworthy is only the first step. The banker must then convince the loan committee.

Bankers who call on retail stores are usually young "business development officers"—they beat the bushes for potential customers, collect loan applications, and bring them back for consideration by the decision makers, the loan committee.

Loan committees are training grounds; they pick apart their apprentices' applications, point out deficiencies, and dwell on every potential pitfall and liability. If our banker can't defend our application adequately, the committee provides further lessons in the form of loan requirements and restrictions, if not outright rejection.

Educate your banker
so the loan committee won't have to.

We can help our banker and our loan by preparing him well, coaching him with answers to the questions he's likely to be asked. If they're complex, we can provide them in writing, review them with him, and make him prove he understands them.

We should encourage him to call us back with questions and offer to review his write-up with him before he submits it (although he's unlikely to agree).

If we don't have confidence in a banker's ability to present our case, we can ask him to introduce us to his boss. When the boss understands and endorses the application, school takes recess.

A good banker won't be your banker long.

Most banks are job carousels. Talented bankers move often, either up or on.

Without some continuity in our banking relationship we're a new applicant at each renewal. Our new banker might understand and support our existing arrangements, but sooner or later one will want to make changes. Gunslinger recruits from other banks often try to prove their worth by increasing rates and fees or tightening terms.

We can establish some continuity by getting to know the people further up. An annual lunch, golf game, or visit with the lending manager and bank management is worth the time, enjoyable or not.

In one stretch of about ten years we had a dozen different bank representatives. Several were young and inexperienced, and undoubtedly represented us poorly to the loan committee, but at least maintained our existing terms.

One young lady, however, was distracted by pregnancy and didn't get the advantageous terms we were accustomed to. After several discussions and negotiations, we told her another bank was offering us what we wanted; she shrugged her shoulders.

Our company had been with this bank for 60 years and this loan was one of the largest and most dependable in their small business lending division. At the last minute we called the bank president to be sure he was aware we were about to change banks. He wasn't; he expressed alarm and immediately approved the terms we wanted.

After this experience we have insisted on annual meetings with the division president and our officer. We give them a tour of our store and then go to lunch to review and discuss the renewal packet we prepare for them.

A banking crisis is always just a personnel change away.

A banker's staid and conservative demeanor often belies some surprisingly arbitrary decisions. Despite ratios and rules, a banker finds ways to rationalize almost any loan that strikes his fancy—or walks away from the most conservative of loans because "it just doesn't feel right."

A new banker means new and different preferences, biases, and decisions. In the most radical cases, he can, seemingly on a whim, abandon entire fields of established lending like auto financing, home mortgages, and retail floor-planning.

It's not uncommon for a new banker to decide he's uncomfortable with a store's finances or plans, or to simply not understand the business model. Suddenly a historical relationship is literally that.

And finding a new bank is far more challenging when it's not by choice. Every potential banker wonders what the previous banker knew.

Financial statements are a banker's reality; everything else is fantasy and excuse.

We might have good reasons for last year's losses, be just around the corner from a breakthrough, have assets worth more than what shows on the balance sheet, and have reliable promises from investors. Great; might as well talk them up.

But we shouldn't expect them to carry much weight. In most cases the loan committee will dismiss them as our hopes and dreams and look to our financial statements for the unvarnished reality.

If our banker tells us he understands what we're saying, we can appreciate his amiability but should suspect his sincerity; in his world, if it's not on the financial statement it isn't worth much. And even if we can convince him, he'll likely struggle convincing the loan committee.

Bankers comprehend ratios, not businesses.

Few bankers understand financial statements from the perspective of operating a business. They don't know how much inventory is appropriate, why receivables are necessary, what margins are needed, what proportion payroll should be to sales, how much advertising is appropriate, what vendor terms are available, etc.

Instead they focus on the application of ratios—debt-to-worth, interest coverage, current ratio, inventory and receivables turnover…. Our financial statements are simply input for their ratios.

An energetic banker will occasionally get out Robert Morris or other analysis reports to compare our numbers to other (sometimes dissimilar) businesses. Such comparisons can be interesting but they tell little of how our businesses actually operate.

> While virtually all bankers use ratios, which ratios they emphasize varies from bank to bank.
>
> We once missed our bank's preferred current ratio for fiscal year-end and they seemed genuinely concerned. What didn't seem to matter to them was that we had made a large cash pre-payment on our long-term bank loan two days before the end of the year.
>
> Next time we'll just pay a little less on the loan and leave a little more in the bank—whatever rings their bell.

Bankers love projections, especially if they prove accurate.

Retailers who make spreadsheet projections of their monthly financial positions give the impression they know what they're doing and where they're going.

The projections might be full of errors or total fictions; initially it doesn't matter since a banker has no way of knowing. Just the fact that someone put the projections together is impressive and reassuring.

But overly optimistic numbers are soon exposed and diminish the credibility of future projections.

Realistic or conservative numbers are easy enough to produce and have many useful purposes —if the cash won't be there to repay the loan, it's helpful to know beforehand.

Loans should fit the business, not just the bank.

Bankers have lots of boxes they like to put loans in: working capital, revolving lines of credit, term, evergreen, amortizing, asset-based, equipment financing, construction, bridge, consolidation, take-out, accounts receivable factoring, business acquisition, unsecured, merchant account cash advance, equipment sale-lease back ....

As long as the amount, terms, and schedule fit our needs it makes little difference what they call it. But when the loan doesn't match our plans, the bank needs to make another box.

We have to make our projections and determine how much we need and when repayment is realistic. Then we have to tell our banker the amounts and the schedule we want and let them work it out.

Early in my career our banker set up our borrowing as a small line of credit and several amortizing loans with alternating renewal dates. He said this was how banks loaned for purposes and assets like ours.

Our projections were for growth that would require increasing loan amounts; their loans were amortizing quickly and required constant renewals. Banking got tiresome quickly.

Eventually we called a meeting, showed them our projections including the loan amounts we'd need for the next few years. We told them we were determined to find borrowing that fit those projections and we hoped it would be with them.

In a few days they came back with a new word for what we wanted and said they could offer it. I don't recall or care what the name is—only that it matches our needs.

MULTIPLE STORES

359

Two stores don't make twice as much.

Opening more stores is just in the DNA of retailers. It's irresistibly logical that a successful store—a proven and profitable retail concept—could be easily replicated. The same products, methods, and operating systems should yield similar results in another location, only with enhanced economies of scale.

It makes so much apparent sense that the question "How many stores do you have?" is almost equivalent to "How successful is your company?" or even "How profitable is your company?"

Ironically they often have the opposite meaning. Second and third stores are rarely as profitable as the original, and often they're losers.

Many store owners with adequate profit breakdowns recognize the source of their reduced profitability and retreat in a few years. Unfortunately most don't have the necessary numbers or aren't willing to swallow their pride; they drag their mistakes behind them like a ball and chain.

Only a few come to grips with the specific differences and added challenges of operating multiple stores, expand their management abilities, and devise methods and formats that will work across multiple locations.

In one of our business sharing groups, those with high profits are sometimes jokingly advised, "You're making too much—you need to open another store."

The most profitable store is the first; the least profitable is the second.

Second stores typically do a fraction of the volume of the original store, and profitability is nowhere close to proportionate—often it's negative.

Apparently no academic study has established the reasons for this, so we can guess with impunity: less experience and dedication in store management, inadequate systems for multiple locations, diminished access to information, less decision and reaction power ....

We often make these challenges even more formidable by designing second stores as smaller versions of the original. The plan of stocking only the top sellers seems logical for increasing efficiency, but backfires when customers bypass the small store for larger selections.

Multiple stores are a separate skill set.

A really strong and profitable retail concept begs replication. If the model is refined and proven, it can work in other locations, multiplying returns.

But an ambitious retailer needs to recognize that operating a chain requires very different skills than building the original.

A single-store operator sees firsthand every day what's broken, what could operate better, who needs help and training, what work is behind, what new opportunities are emerging, etc. He spends his time fine-tuning the operation, helping staff develop to potential, and exploring new opportunities. He teaches by example, shares experience anecdotally, and motivates with personal interaction.

A multiple-store owner doesn't see the problems and opportunities directly; he has to infer them from numbers and reports, and attempt to influence them remotely. He experiences the front line less often, and spends much of his time in an office removed from the stores.

His management tools include a strong information system, standardized operating systems, formal training, carefully designed incentive systems, planograms, secret shoppers, periodic inspections, and audits. When results are inadequate he rarely has time to investigate the causes; he replaces personnel until he gets better results.

The goal—a smoothly operating retail store—is the same for single or multiple stores, but the methods and tools used to accomplish it are totally different.

In musical instrument retailing, successful single store operators often expand to two or three stores, at which point their profitability declines enough to dissuade them from further expansion. (The fact that the market isn't flooded by continually expanding retailers is convincing evidence in itself of the declining profitability.)

Unfortunately most musical instrument retailers can't or don't trace the source of their decline to the added stores. As a result most m.i. "chains" stall at several stores.

Size is the adversary of excellence.

Most of us know how our stores should operate. The challenge of retailing isn't recognizing what's right, it's getting so many details right at once. That's full-time employment for almost all of us. If we get most of the details right, we make a profit; miss more than a few and we take a loss.

Each additional store multiplies the details we're responsible for and divides our time to tend to them. Distance increases the challenge, not just of correcting problems but also of seeing what needs correcting, and knowing how to correct it and when it's corrected.

Once in a business sharing group we charted the efficiency of companies against their number of locations. The correlation was virtually perfect; the more locations, the lower were profits as a percentage of sales, return on assets, sales to payroll, sales per square foot, sales per employee, gross margin per employee, and profit per store.

The model stores for efficiency were, consistently, large single-store operations.

That's not to say the total profits of the single stores were higher than the chains. Since the chains' total sales were sometimes many times higher, their total profits occasionally were, too—just not proportionately so and not nearly as much as might be expected.

The large chains also seemed to be in wider disarray, have more threatening challenges, live closer to the edge financially, bounce between profit and loss, and were often fighting desperately to solve some operational or personnel problem that was critical mostly due to its size.

Only simple, highly profitable concepts can endure multiple locations.

Multi-store models must be simple enough to replicate easily and profitable enough to make up for their inefficiencies.

Stores with complex operations have too many moving parts to reproduce dependably. They require experienced and motivated employees—a resource both rare and precious.

Marginally profitable models are too vulnerable to the inevitable inefficiencies. When a store lets any of the hundreds of details slip through the cracks, even temporarily, thin profits turn into losses.

Effective multi-store operators prune and fine-tune their concepts to maximum profitability, then distill them to simple systems that can be taught quickly and don't veer off course easily.

Great managers are the vital but elusive ingredient.

Among the many challenges of operating multiple stores, finding appropriate management tops most retailers' lists. Unless the business concept is exceptionally simple, the manager is the single most critical component—and unfortunately the rarest of talents.

Applicants and experience are plentiful, and a company can provide training, business philosophy, and operational guidance. But unless there is a powerful, innate drive deep within the store manager, results will be disappointing.

During the years we operated four stores, we experienced the effects of managers many times.

Average managers maintained neat stores, hired reliable people, served walk-in customers adequately, and were congenial to work with. Their stores hovered around breakeven.

Good managers stocked and arranged their stores to maximize sales, chose people for their sales potential, taught proper techniques by example, inspired helpful attitudes and contagious determination, were proactive in attracting customers, and fought for business. They were sometimes quirky but they made their stores work. These managers were highly profitable—and in very short supply.

When we exchanged a good manager for an average one and vice versa, store results quickly reversed.

A manager's incentive
is never as great as the owner's.

Even the most enthusiastic and responsible store manager can't have the same commitment to a business as the person who conceived it, nursed it to its current success, has his name attached to it, and has his life savings invested in it.

Financial incentives are effective motivators, but their range for managers (typically commissions and bonuses to supplement a salary) is never as wide as for a store owner (bankruptcy to independent wealth).

A business is often consuming for its owner. In addition to spending the majority of his waking hours working in it, he spends much of his time off rehashing decisions and events, studying and worrying about possibilities, and considering or planning improvements.

A store manager, no matter how motivated, is rarely so tied to the business; for him there's life outside and beyond the company.

A manager proposes his ideas
while an owner implements his.

A store owner has the luxury of making immediate decisions. He can take action as soon as he discovers a profitable opportunity, senses a need to change policy, detects a shift in product demand, envisions an improvement in facilities, notices a maintenance need, perceives advantages to changing or adding personnel ....

A store manager typically must prepare and make his case to upper management. If his vision is not shared, it's not only his ideas that are killed but often his motivation.

Information is understanding, inspiration, and motivation.

Financial details, operating results, and philosophies are seldom as available to store managers as to ownership or even headquarters staff. It's difficult for a manager to understand which things to do when he can't see or feel their impact on the company.

Managers of stores also are often less plugged-in to the rest of the industry. They typically don't attend industry conventions and meetings, don't see as many manufacturers' reps, and don't meet many other store managers. They're often insulated from industry news, sometimes not even receiving the trade journals.

Their ideas and inspiration are limited by the indirect and filtered information they get through ownership or upper management.

Smaller stores create smaller sales and much smaller profits.

Second stores are usually reduced versions of the original store.

Customers will shop for inexpensive items in a small store, but they will drive to a larger selection for bigger purchases. Even when a small store has exactly the product the customer will buy, he often won't buy until he's seen a broader selection. As a result, small stores typically get proportionally fewer of the large sales.

Small stores are also handicapped in that their staffs must be generalists. Salespeople in small stores see too few of each customer type to develop specialized knowledge and expertise, and they get fewer opportunities to practice and hone their sales skills and develop confidence.

As a result a few large stores are often a more profitable investment than many small stores.

We constantly felt the effects of smaller size with our three "branch" stores.

We knew the size of our displays was critical since, from the customers' perspective, they were the selection. When a dozen pianos, fifteen band instruments, forty guitars, and a few drum sets proved not enough on display, we built stores without stockrooms and displayed everything we had.

Still we attracted mostly the small sales, while customers traveled to a bigger store—ours or someone else's—to make bigger purchases. Even when we stocked the stores with exactly the products they would eventually buy, they wouldn't buy them from a small selection.

> Bigger is often better in retail, but there is a limit.
>
> One of the most notable examples of too big was Tandy's chain of electronics superstores, Incredible Universe. Opened in 1992 with great fanfare, the 180,000 sq. ft. gigastores carried 85,000 SKUs. Chairman John Roach predicted there would be Incredible Universe stores in every major market in the U.S.
>
> Sales proved well below expectations and by 1996 Tandy had seen enough. It closed all seventeen Incredible Universe stores to "focus on its RadioShack stores and maximizing cashflow."
>
> "Bigger is better" doesn't always mean biggest is best.

Chains are retail's high-stakes gamble.

A large, smoothly operating, profitable chain is a thing of beauty, a tribute to its management, and a golden goose to its owners and investors. But before betting the farm on a chain a retailer needs to think through the odds and obstacles.

It can be done—it's been proven in almost every field. And advantages never seen before are available today in modern information systems, access to large pools of capital, and methods of communication.

But managing the innumerable facets of large chain retailing is a juggling act mastered by few and rarely for long.

Chains occasionally collapse, almost as quickly as they spring up. Retail is in constant evolution and multiple layers of management, inflexible systems, entrenched policies and culture, high leverage, etc., make adapting even more challenging. New competitors, unencumbered by legacy methods and equipment, and agile smaller retailers constantly raise the bar and change the game.

The rewards are outsize but so are the risks.

> Among the large retail chains that folded in 2007-2008 were Circuit City, CompUSA, Bombay, Linens 'n Things, Mervyn's, Sharper Image, Tweeter, and Woolworth's. Although their concepts were once cutting edge and highly profitable, they apparently weren't able to adapt quickly enough as the market and competitors changed.

Building a chain isn't for everyone.

Even if we have a concept that's strong, profitable, and simple enough to work across many stores, we still have to ask ourselves if it's the right strategy for us. Despite the common assumption, a large chain is not the ultimate goal of all retailers.

Among those to whom a chain appeals are those in quest of a financial jackpot; multiple stores ups the ante, making fortunes possible, even as it decreases the odds.

Others relish the challenge of creating something extraordinary or the high-stakes competition of a broader field.

But many feel expanding and refining an existing store offers more than enough opportunity for income as well as more predictable returns on capital, time, and effort.

And some simply prefer the daily routine of local retailing, the community interaction and involvement, and the option to transfer the business to future generations.

ACQUISITIONS

371

Buying market share is often cheaper than fighting for it.

If we're really better than our competitors, we can beat them and win market share, right? So why buy a competitor's store when we can build our own?

Because, unless our offering is leaps and bounds ahead of our competitors', picking up market share takes time and money.

Competitor battles take a toll on all market participants and the market as a whole. Price wars create unrealistic customer expectations and often depress prices long term. When competition gets nasty, competitors damage each other's reputations and leave deep scars in a local market.

If a competitor is already in place and the pieces are a reasonably good fit, buying him can be a shortcut to increased profits.

The value of an acquisition
is often not the store itself.

Real estate seldom has much value in an acquisition; most property is leased, presumably at market rates. Some stores' names would appear to be valuable, yet acquirers rarely keep them long. The store's policies and operating systems are rarely an attraction; they're among the first things to be changed.

Inventory and receivables sometimes contribute value in an acquisition, but only when they're bought at bargain prices.

In many acquisitions most of the value is in the people. Proven salespeople can add big numbers to the bottom line, and their contacts and relationships allow them to begin contributing immediately. Experienced managers can bring not only abilities but proven promotional and operational ideas, industry contacts, and often product and sourcing relationships.

And sometimes there's value simply in having the competitor exit, especially if he has significant market share, has been a worthy opponent, or has depressed prices.

373

Stores that aren't for sale often get sold.

Some store owners haven't thought about selling but would gladly entertain the idea if presented. Others would like to sell but don't want to advertise and don't know how to find a buyer. And some haven't bothered looking because they feel no one would be interested.

Many have fought long and hard for small returns and are tired of the battle; if they saw a way out, they'd likely take it. Others have faced recent frustrations in personnel, banking, taxes, supplier relationships, key customers, sales declines, or any of the myriad other challenges of retailing; they'd welcome the opportunity to turn their problems over to someone else.

Even when a store owner decides to retire, he typically takes years to get around to it; a simple exit plan accompanied by a check might be all the encouragement he needs.

> My brother regularly calls our competitors to ask how it's going and remind them to call us if they become interested in selling.
>
> The owners typically dismiss the idea off-hand — "We're doing fine; not interested in selling." But a surprising number call back months or years later. Typically some crisis has arisen and they're not as fond of the business as they were previously.
>
> We want them to call us when they first entertain the thought of selling. We hate finding out after they've sold the store to a new, young, energetic competitor with lots of pricing and expense lessons to learn.

374

Profitable stores aren't for sale.

When an owner is willing to sell his store, it's almost always because the store is losing money. He's tired, running out of cash, and has lost hope. (That's the meaning of "I'm just ready to do something else.")

He'd like to just walk away but he's responsible for a lease and needs to liquidate his inventory and other assets. He'd love to find a buyer who will simply take it all off his hands so he can move on.

The rare exception is when a store owner develops a serious health problem or dies. Then a profitable store must be sold, sometimes at a reasonable price.

375

Unprofitable stores are often better buys.

When we buy a company at its highest sales and profits, we pay top price. In many cases there's little improvement we can bring to its operations; indeed if the previous owner was good, it can be difficult to maintain the existing levels.

An unprofitable store often offers better opportunities. Sometimes we can see its problems, have dealt with them before, and know the solutions. Occasionally they're as simple as inappropriate pricing, poor location, wrong inventory, inefficient operating systems, poorly chosen personnel, or ineffective incentive systems.

Surprisingly often a few products, departments, or services are losing money while the rest struggle to make up. That fix is quick and simple: eliminate the losers and emphasize the winners.

And sometimes the store's inventory, receivables, and people are more valuable individually than as an operating store. Often they can be profitably folded into existing operations, and the lease subbed or bought out.

A competitor for sale is always worth a look.

When a competitor asks if we're interested in buying, it's almost always worth the time to talk. Even if we feel a deal is unlikely we can learn about market share, special niches, unusual operating methods, good personnel, plans and options, and occasionally some valuable industry scuttlebutt. A store owner who has decided to leave the market can be surprisingly candid.

Sometimes there are ways we can help him leave—buying some merchandise, offering to sell remaining inventory on consignment, helping him find a liquidator, suggesting ways to settle with vendors, offering to employ him and/or key employees .... After all, we're on the same team now—we both want him out.

377

A store's asking price and value are seldom related.

Sellers almost never know how to value their businesses and many seem to resist any logical calculations. They usually have blue-sky expectations based on the years of sweat and effort they've put in.

Most owners will accept a reasonable price only when under pressure to sell—the company is losing money, creditors are closing in, health problems have developed, all other options have been exhausted, etc. And that often takes some time after initial discussions.

378

When the emotion clears a store's value is simple math.

Perhaps the most common impediment to selling a store is that either the buyer or the seller (and sometimes both) doesn't know how to calculate a fair price. Not until both parties have a realistic idea of its value is an agreement possible.

The calculations aren't difficult. For example:

1. Average the profits of the last three years.

2. Adjust the profits by what a hired manager would make in salary and benefits.

3. Multiply the adjusted average profit by four to six, depending upon the risk of the business relative to other potential investments.

When the above calculation produces a value significantly less than the book value of the company (total assets less liabilities), a sale of the assets might bring more.

At one time we were getting so many calls to buy small stores in our area that we wrote out the calculations to leave with them.

If we're able to get together on a purchase, here's how we'd calculate the price:

1. *From your store's income tax returns for the last 3 years, we'd calculate its average profit.*
2. *If your salary was more than $60k, we'd add the excess to the average profit; if it was less, we'd subtract the difference.*
3. *We'd multiply the adjusted average profit by 4 to get the net value of the business.*

Alternately we could buy the accounts receivable and inventory from you. For inventory in saleable condition we can give you 50% of the current Blue Book wholesale value; for accounts receivable that are current we can give you 70% of the outstanding balances.

Feel free to think about these figures a few days and then we can talk.

We sometimes adjust the numbers depending on how interested we are in the business and how much we want them out of the market.

In almost every case the seller has chosen the AR/inventory method. (If the store was profitable it wouldn't be for sale, right?) The profit calculations just dispel blue sky dreams.

379

"Synergy" is the delusion of business egos.

Contrary to initial enthusiasm, very few store acquisitions meet profitability expectations as ongoing operations. Sellers ask too much and buyers overestimate their abilities to improve sales and efficiencies or even to continue operating at the same level.

There should indeed be synergies, including economies of scale, increased buying power, sharing of best practices, and advertising economies.

But there are challenges too, including especially keeping good managers, communications, access to information, decision power, and motivation. The challenges almost always prove more formidable than the synergies.

Perhaps the most prominent example of the folly of synergies was the rollup fad of the '90s.

"Rollups" were acquisitions of many small private businesses to create one large public company that could benefit from such synergies as group buying and sourcing, sophisticated information systems, sharing of best practices, professional management, and access to low-cost investment for expansion.

Waste Management was one of the earliest, buying up independent trash haulers. WM stock was a high-flier for the first few years while there were many independent trash haulers to acquire. During these years WM's focus was on growth through acquisition, and efficient management of the acquired companies seemed hardly a concern.

Those who engineered the rollup made a fortune from the run-up of the stock. But once the acquisitions were made and the operating challenges became visible, the stock plummeted and stockholders, including those who traded their privately-owned companies for Waste Management stock, lost fortunes.

Video stores, funeral homes, heat & air services, office supplies, used cars, and many more rollups that followed suffered substantially the same fate—not only did the "synergies" not add profits but the colossus struggled to maintain pre-merger results.

Apparently the concept of synergy is easier to sell than to execute.

FINANCIAL MANAGEMENT

380

He who reads the map is the leader.

Financial statements are the best indicators we have of where our businesses are, have been, and are going. They are our most powerful tool for measuring results, spotting trouble, and projecting trends.

An owner or CEO can hire the ability to prepare the financial statements but he can't delegate responsibility for reading, interpreting, and acting on them. He has to have a clear picture of the company's position, understand the value of contributions and the costs of inadequacies, and assess the risks and rewards of opportunities. From these he chooses directions, sets goals, and enlists support.

A leader who doesn't comprehend his financial statements is groping and guessing, and luck runs out quickly with so many wrong paths beckoning.

Financial insight isn't enough to ensure that a store is successful, but lack of it is enough to ensure that a store is not.

Some years ago I was friends with a young second-generation owner of a very successful and respected musical instrument store. He was an extraordinary marketer and a personable manager, but he had no background in or knowledge of financial management.

He recognized that shortcoming and thus offered a young CPA a key management position in the company. The accountant could create financial statements and prepare tax forms, but he had no background in running a retail business.

On a flight layover my brother and I stopped to visit our friend at his store. He and the financial manager gave us a tour and laid out their plans. They were "building the financial engine for a thirty-to-forty store chain." They leased warehouse space, bought a huge computer system, and hired personnel to support sales many times their current level.

We were truly frightened by the plan. Although they had three or four successful stores, they didn't have a store model strong enough that new locations would be instantly profitable. Nor did they have the equity or financial resources to sustain so much infrastructure until new stores became profitable.

We raised enough questions and objections to risk our welcome but to no avail. Maybe it was already too late, as they had committed to too many expenses.

In less than a year the bank pulled the plug, and all the efforts of family, friends, and previous managers couldn't save it. A thirty-year-old respected and historically profitable company was dissolved into bankruptcy, all lost their jobs, and the guarantors lost their homes.

The demise of this company was almost surely the CEO's failure to understand financial statements and projections and to recognize the CPA's advice as naïve and inexperienced.

The past, present, and possible are all in the numbers.

Historical numbers define where we've been; they show us the effectiveness of what we've done and help us recognize and rectify our mistakes.

Current numbers show us what we have to work with and help us assess what we can afford to risk.

Projected numbers let us weigh our options and opportunities, foresee challenges, choose our directions, and set our strategies.

Our numbers are the most objective descriptions we have of our stores and contain far more insights and opportunities than we'll ever extract.

Projections are experience made affordable.

Almost any scenario can be projected, much quicker and at far less expense than living it.

Projections show us what results we can expect from store expansions, price wars, recessions, lay-offs, new or diminished competition, discounting, changing merchandise, and most other potentialities. Even when they don't lead us to radically new and different strategies, they help us understand the possibilities—and that goes a long way in relieving anxiety and creating confidence.

Calculated outcomes are seldom what we expect. Sometimes they disappoint by showing an exciting plan to be hardly worth the effort; occasionally they uncover surprising profits in unsuspected opportunities; and not uncommonly, they warn us away from tempting catastrophes.

Committing to expensive long-term ventures and strategies without projecting their potential and probable outcomes means spending years of our lives and incomes discovering what a few simple projections might have revealed.

At the annual NAMM convention I often use a privately-owned business center for printing services. While I'm used to the seemingly high prices in most of these shops, this one raises the bar.

But I noticed that after a few years most of the other business centers in the area were gone; this one remains, offering ready and efficient service on up-to-date equipment.

It occurred to me that while the other stores had set their prices by what customers expected to pay, this one set rates according to their projections of what it would take to survive and thrive.

The best gut decision is to do the numbers first.

A "feel" for financial results is rarely accurate and is sometimes diametrically opposed to reality. Important decisions made on feel are more often catastrophic than heroic.

Retail profits are a small percentage of revenue. The balance between sales and expense is delicate and easily upset; off-the-cuff estimates almost always omit expenses that tip the scale the wrong way.

Decisions of consequence deserve solid numbers. Yes, this takes time and effort—but nowhere near as much as living through and recovering from bad "gut" decisions.

Leverage limits reaction time.

According to many real estate gurus, leverage is magic dust that creates riches, as if getting deeply into debt is all we have to do to become fabulously wealthy. They don't mention that it's also the main highway to bankruptcy.

There's a place for leverage but, like most things in life, it requires moderation; and like most things in business, it requires careful planning and analysis.

When a retail concept is strong, involves tolerable risk, and promises returns on growth that exceed borrowing costs, leverage makes sense.

The downside to borrowing is, of course, that the money must be repaid, whether or not plans work out. The amount of leverage we have determines how much time and room we have to maneuver in our adjustments. A store with high debt and modest equity has small leeway for mistakes and little time to correct them.

A little success creates a lot of overhead.

When times are good we tend to add people, give raises, lease more space, add more inventory, upgrade equipment, create new bonuses, and increase benefits. The moves make sense when sales are growing.

But they are also long-term commitments to continuing expenses that are hard to shed if necessary later. And they set precedents and establish an operational philosophy that becomes entrenched.

When we hire more people, work expands and we soon wonder how we ever got it done without them—indeed we often can't again. Making leasehold improvements, replacing computers and software, and buying new equipment are paid for with today's cash, but the depreciation expenses drag down profitability for some years into the future.

Good results also allow us to overlook weak departments and locations, excuse poor performance, and put off needed but unpleasant changes.

Fat and happy is often dangerous and temporary; many retailers prefer lean and mean as both safer and more efficient.

Inadequate financing is more consequence of failure than cause.

A favorite "reason" for business failure is inadequate financing. Isn't that like listing "heart stoppage" as a cause of death?

In most cases cash shortages aren't the reason for failure but the result. A successful business has many possible sources of cash; a failing business finds its sources dried up.

Sometimes improper management causes the failure, sometimes the plan isn't sound, and sometimes execution is inadequate. Occasionally conditions beyond the control of the business simply change.

In rare cases more money could save a business; in most cases it would only prolong the inevitable and multiply the damage.

One of our previous competitors blamed the demise of his company on his inability to collect some receivables—if a few large customers had paid him on time he could have paid his bills and continued operating.

The debts weren't unusual; they were the normal costs and frustrations of doing business. The store had been in a slide for years. Collecting those debts might have delayed his fate, but not for long.

Patient growth,
impatient profitability.

We have an innate tendency to focus on growth as the Holy Grail and answer to all our profitability challenges. If we can just sell a little more, we'll be able to cover our expenses and maybe even make a little money.

But growth is as often the way into trouble as the way out. Chasing sales with high expenses and insufficient margins only increases our problems; more sales bring more losses, often in the same old proportions.

In most cases the solution to unprofitability is to step off the sales treadmill and fix the business—the sooner the better. After it's running smoothly and profitably we can grow again.

Growth can wait; profitability cannot.

A good effort makes money in almost
any field—but not as much.

We can add a product, fix an underperforming area, or expand into any new field we like, and with enough effort probably make a profit at it.

Finding opportunities is not the challenge—they're abundant. Choosing the best is.

Our time and effort are limited and where to apply them deserves careful consideration. Spreading ourselves thin over many activities or ventures is a formula for anemic profits or losses in all of them.

Many products and fields have excess competition or low demand; regardless of the time and effort we invest in them, our returns will be small.

Contribution margin is a cop-out.

Most managerial accounting books teach an accounting format that tracks sales and expenses individually for stores and departments only as far as their specific direct expenses; what's left is called their contribution margins. All stores' and departments' contribution margins are then lumped together and the company's general and administrative expenses are deducted to get a company net profit.

The problem is that, while stores and departments may show positive contribution margins, they're often insufficient to cover their fair shares of G&A expense. Even when every store and every department has a positive contribution margin, the company as a whole can be losing money. Such accounting leads management, including especially store and department managers, to believe a store or department is doing well when in reality it's not paying its own way.

Contribution margin is not profit, and accounting that stops mid-way through expenses deceives those who rely on it.

Increased gross margin is the usual remedy for anemic profits.

The solution for underperforming stores is often simple: Raising prices, even a few percentage points, would multiply profits and create precious working capital.

But every store owner and manager has an arsenal of reasons why he can't, almost all of which translate as, "We'll lose sales."

Yes, that's correct—we lose some of the sales that have been losing money. Total sales will be smaller, and we have to adjust expenses to match. But the volume that remains makes money.

The formula is no secret. Why are we so afraid of it?

Coffee shops traditionally haven't been models of profitability. Many are remnants of another era, seemingly operated more out of habit and community than income. Others are used as loss leaders for businesses with better returns.

Then Starbucks created a new model.

Who hasn't marveled at Starbucks' pricing? It keeps plenty of customers away. But those who buy anyway have helped build a chain of legendary profits and growth.

Turnaround plans aren't innovative.

Getting out of financial trouble is always unpleasant but seldom ingenious. The basic steps are:

1. Correct the books. Troubled companies rarely have accurate financial statements. Verify all numbers on the balance sheet, including especially receivables, inventory, and payables, and create accurate income statements. Until we know where we are, we can't know what to fix and when we've fixed it.

2. Determine which activities are making money and which are losing. Divide the financial statement by locations and departments, and allocate expenses all the way to the bottom line.

3. Create a plan to get rid of the losers. We can't go soft here; we get support to fix it once but not twice. We have to do the whole job the first time.

4. Get buy-in from managers, employees, vendors, and creditors.

5. Execute the plan quickly, boldly, and resolutely. We're heroes if we follow through, misguided losers if we back off.

Turnaround plans don't include radical new concepts. The ship must be righted and stabilized before it sets off in new directions and on new ventures.

Trouble plans need conservative sales projections and aggressive expense cuts, not vice versa.

When our stores hit hard times, we resist the solution. Instead of cutting expenses enough to stop the bleeding, we project sales increases sufficient to bail us out. When the sales don't materialize, we project them again, dismissing the lesson as no more than a temporary setback.

Sales projections should match sales trends—no hoping, no rationalization, no BS. Then expenses must be cut far enough to make that level profitable.

Decreasing sales can be profitable if expenses decrease in step.

Sales declines need not be a death knell. After all, we got by with lower sales on the way up.

The key, of course, is keeping expenses in line with sales. But that's not so easy to do. When we don't recognize and project where we're going, our expenses inevitably stay behind the sales trend—we adjust this year's expenses to match last year's sales, and the losses follow us in every step down.

Necessities are luxuries
in the wake of losses.

When the bottom line turns red, business shifts into crisis mode. Everything we "need" moves down the priority list to make room for the one thing we need most—profitability. It's all hands on deck, with one unified and urgent focus—save the ship from sinking.

Leasehold improvements, equipment upgrades, expansions, much advertising, personnel additions, raises, travel—all must wait until profit returns.

Profitability is survival—the sine qua non of retailing.

There is no such thing as a fixed expense.

Any expense can be reduced or eliminated, usually much faster than we assume.

The concept of fixed and variable expenses comes primarily from manufacturing. Raw material and labor are variable expenses because they increase and decrease with production. Machinery is a fixed expense; the cost of buying and installing a machine is the same whether we use the machine or not.

Retail has no "fixed" expenses. Payroll, retail's largest expense, is not—people can be redeployed in seconds, and unemployed if necessary. Rent is not—space can be used for other purposes, or subleased or sold. Even equipment leasing and depreciation are not, as equipment can be sold when necessary.

Reducing salespeople reduces expenses —and sometimes sales.

Payroll is a retailer's largest expense so reducing it is a key element of virtually every turnaround plan.

We often feel a reduced sales force could handle the existing customer flow. If the staff is primarily clerks, that's probably true, at least for the short term.

But when sales depend on salesperson initiative, relationship-building, or follow-up, reducing the sales staff is sometimes poor economy. The loss of sales often more than offsets the reduction in payroll.

In our musical instrument store we've found we can operate with fewer cashiers with little effect on sales. Most customers will wait a minute or two to pay for their purchases if they have to.

But reducing piano salespeople has a very different effect. For example, if we have two salespeople consistently selling $600,000 each and we lose one, the remaining one doesn't sell $1,200,000, but $900,000. Since our salespeople are paid a small salary plus commissions, the expense savings of one less is small but the gross margin reduction is huge—terrible economy, capable of creating a downward spiral.

Perhaps busy salespeople aren't able to provide as much attention and follow-up. Or maybe each salesperson brings or makes his or her own group of outside contacts and sales. Maybe salespeople just get tired and aren't as sharp. Some might even say a salesman doesn't work as hard once he's reached his personal goals.

397

*What's called genius
is really determination.*

There is no standard pattern for great retailers; they come in all varieties of intelligence, physique, education, background, culture, and style.

Some are bright, others seem slow to get it; some have Ivy League diplomas, others have GEDs; some are polished, others have mud on their boots; some are eloquent speakers, others afraid of crowds. Many are odd in some ways, like athletes, performers, and musicians who devote their lives to a single pursuit.

But there is one characteristic all successful retailers have in common: powerful and unwavering determination to make their stores right. It's the essential ingredient, incalculably more important than the brains, education, contacts, and lucky circumstances that so often get the credit.

Perhaps the greatest benefit of serving as chairman of NAMM, the International Music Products Association, was the opportunity to get to know the heads of companies like Steinway, Guitar Center, Yamaha, Gibson, Fender, Peavey, Roland, and Conn/Selmer.

I expected these people to somehow be super-human—tall, intelligent, worldly, profound, charismatic, handsome, etc. What I found surprised me. They came in all shapes and sizes, some hardly attractive. Many were street smart rather than college-educated. While most could convey their ideas, many were socially awkward or so narrowly focused as to be oblivious to all else but their businesses.

However there was an overriding trait within each of them: every one was extremely focused on results, driven and determined to achieve his goals.

The qualities I expected would surely have been helpful but apparently not at all necessary—and they ranked way down the list from determination.

"My God-given talent is my ability to stick with something longer than anyone else."

—Herschel Walker

Education isn't critical but willingness to learn is.

No education can prepare us for all the situations we face in retailing. Even if we could memorize exactly what's needed in today's environment, it wouldn't be useful long. Education is valuable, but not because it teaches us specific job skills; because it teaches us how to learn.

We don't have to know everything, but we do have to be willing and eager to learn what we need whenever we discover we need it.

Education is a head-start, but in the retail marathon learning along the way easily overtakes it.

> "For students starting a four year technical degree, over half of what they learn in their first year of study will be outdated by their third year of study."
>
> **—Karl Fisch, Scott McLeod, & Jeff Brenman as popularized in the "Did You Know" video**

Leadership is a role but not a job description.

A leader chooses the direction and goals for his company, then organizes the company to best pursue them. Organization entails structuring jobs and functions to fit the abilities and personalities available to him. And such job design includes his own; he must shape his job to make use of his own special skills and abilities, and delegate wherever he perceives his weaknesses.

Retailers who are charismatic often serve as the public faces of their stores; many others shun the spotlight and appoint staffers to public roles.

Some retailers like formulating detailed plans; others prefer broad strokes and strategies, relying on staff to work out the details.

Some enjoy making deals and working out compromises; others lack the patience and diplomacy for negotiation and assign it to more social personalities.

The essential of leadership is choosing what's to be done and organizing the company to do it—not necessarily doing it ourselves.

Neither Benjamin Franklin nor Thomas Jefferson was a good public speaker.

Franklin rarely gave speeches at all, often asking colleagues to read what he had written; the few speeches he gave were memorable mostly for his weak delivery. Virtually all the influence he exerted was with a pen or printers' ink.

Jefferson seldom uttered more than a few sentences in public meetings. Despite doing most of the writing of the Declaration of Independence, he hardly spoke while the Continental Congress debated and mangled his work. His inaugural address could barely be heard beyond the first few rows.

Yet the leadership of these two giants guided the U.S. through its most tentative and vulnerable period, shaping not only the U.S. government but subsequent democracies around the world.

Strength in others isn't a threat but an opportunity.

Not everyone wants to lead a company—many have other interests and priorities, are adverse to the risks, or simply don't have the personality for leadership.

But these people often have impressive skills, knowledge, and abilities that can be valuably employed to everyone's benefit. They depend on someone else to put together an organization that can translate those skills and abilities into profit and provide them an income.

The smart leader surrounds himself with people with greater knowledge and skills, puts them to maximum use, gratefully acknowledges their contributions, and compensates them fairly for their efforts.

401

Having the answers isn't critical, but recognizing them is.

We don't have to have all the specialized expertise our business needs. We only have to know where to find it and be able to distinguish the feasible and helpful from the unrealistic and harmful.

Professional advisors (CPAs, lawyers, bankers, systems consultants, etc.) are experts in their fields because they specialize—they spend their careers immersed in the details. But that specialization is at the expense of other knowledge and skills; they are not retailers and cannot understand retailing like a retailer.

We have to choose our advisors and advice carefully, and discriminately meld the advice into our business in the correct proportions and with the appropriate emphasis.

Following advice because "My accountant said ..." is foolish and dangerous. A good advisor only points out the considerations; a good retailer weighs them and decides whether and how to integrate them.

Results depend more on what you do than on what the environment does.

The economy, inflation, gas prices, exchange rates, and government regulation are among the many factors regularly cited and blamed for business results. Investors gamble fortunes on trends in demographics, construction, real estate, currencies, and the like, almost as if they alone were responsible for the success of the businesses they invest in.

Occasionally a trend is powerful enough to completely change the potential of a company. Digital photography's effect on Kodak's film business and computers' effect on Smith-Corona's typewriter business are examples.

But most of the news we read has relatively little effect on our businesses compared to our daily efforts. It provides topics of conversation between businessmen and excuses for those with poor results. But for those who hustle and innovate, outside influences are at most just potholes and speed bumps; they occasionally slow us down or divert us but they don't stop us.

Good fortune in retail is never luck, but determined execution of a reasonable plan.

"Right place, right time" is a persistent myth to explain business success.

Timing can impede or assist a business idea, but success isn't a lotto jackpot, bestowed randomly on a surprised and undeserving recipient.

The essential ingredient is always someone who recognized an opportunity, believed in it passionately, and pushed it through against odds and obstacles that deterred countless others to whom the idea also occurred.

Rather than a sudden stroke of luck success is most often the sum of countless small steps, forward and back—incremental progress in a determined journey toward a dreamed-of destination.

404

There's more than one right answer.

Retailing is not a math problem with one absolute and incontrovertible solution. Business situations have many facets, markets are diverse, and customers have different needs. Sometimes an innovative and unexpected approach is the differentiation a store needs.

The plan with the best chance of success is almost always the one management believes in passionately enough to make it work.

My greatest disappointment with business school was that there were no "correct" answers to case studies. (Case studies are real-life business situations including a management dilemma, laid out in multi-page detail.)

After working sometimes 10-20 hours crafting what I believed to be the best solution, naturally I wanted to know how I'd done. But there were no answers offered, no red-ink corrections, no upside-down answer codes in the back of the book—not even teachers' guides available surreptitiously. And no savvy business professor would ever risk his own solution; most subscribed to Socratic teaching, offering only questions about yours.

The point of the exercise was simply to think through all of the situations' aspects and commit to a plan of action. If the premises weren't totally off-base and the commitment was strong enough, it would likely work.

"There are no rules here—we're trying to accomplish something."

—Thomas Edison

405

To find two things that work, try ten.

Experience helps us rule out ideas that have little chance, but only trial separates what's left into winners and nice tries.

Trying many ideas adds to our experience base and often shows us what could work if we tweaked it or combined it with other ideas and lessons.

Successful retailers aren't successful in everything they do. They just try enough things to find some that work.

> It's not so much that we don't make mistakes, but that we learn from them.

406

All great innovations begin as insurrections.

No worthwhile change in retailing can be accomplished without offending someone. People to be displaced and businesses to be disrupted can be fierce adversaries. Those who will benefit most from the change often don't recognize its benefits and cling to the habits they're comfortable with.

Yet we can't make progress without change.

Ultimately a good idea is irresistible and the market is the final arbiter of its value.

> "And it ought to be remembered that there is nothing more difficult to take in hand, more perilous to conduct, or more uncertain in its success, than to take the lead in the introduction of a new order of things. Because the innovator has for enemies all those who have done well under the old conditions, and lukewarm defenders in those who may do well under the new."
>
> **—Machiavelli**

Change is its own reason for change.

Sometimes it's helpful to shake things up. Employees get bored and complacent, operations become mindless routines, displays and décor get stale, enthusiasm slips into habit, and customer allegiance settles into expectation.

Novelty and innovation keep business fresh and interesting. Continuous experimentation and improvement form a culture of excitement and passion.

In the late 1920s, psychologists conducting experiments at Western Electric's Hawthorne plant found that when they increased lighting levels in the factory, worker morale and productivity went up. Understandable. But when they decreased lighting levels, productivity increased again.

Similar experiments with room temperature and rest periods were conducted; each change, whatever its direction, produced, at least temporarily, measurable improvements in morale and productivity.

You're never really as smart as when business is good, nor as dumb as when business is bad.

It's easy to forget how small the margin is between success and failure.

A hot new product, an innovative promotion, or a new twist to an old marketing concept can reap sudden and unexpected rewards. Profits fund store and operational improvements as well as experiments with fun new ideas, attracting the attention of customers, peers, and the industry. Everyone is eager to listen and learn the secret of the Midas touch.

But new competition, changing technology, a shift in fashions, or simply overlooking any of the fundamentals of retailing can reverse fortunes quickly. Suddenly everything that worked so smoothly and easily is fraught with problems. Red numbers suck the fun out of retailing.

Pride has a painful inverse in humility.

The '70s and '80s saw a tiresome influx of books on Japanese management. Certainly some good ideas were extracted from Japanese business, but who didn't grow weary of hearing how brilliant Japanese managers were and how clueless American managers were in comparison?

Wage increases, shifting exchange rates, recession, and other factors soon created decades of economic malaise in Japan. Today anyone who wanted a book on Japanese management would have to search the bargain bins of used bookstores.

STRATEGIC MANAGEMENT

409

Hope is not a plan.

We wouldn't get in our cars and pull out of our driveways without knowing where we're going. Yet we sometimes work for years and gamble our company's equity and survival without knowing where we're going and how we'll get there.

"Just keep doing what we're doing" might be a reasonable plan if we've just come off a successful year, the market isn't changing, competitors aren't catching up, and we've got plenty of equity to continue the trend. But that's not a description of retailing.

We have too much at risk to trust luck. We need realistic projections of where we're going, a strategy to get there, and contingency plans for coping with the potential challenges along the way.

> "If you don't know where you're going, any road will do."
>
> **—Alice in Wonderland**

Many can ride, but one must drive.

Every company needs a person who sees the aerial view, chooses the direction and goals, analyzes the map and progress on it, and makes needed course adjustments— someone who, at least periodically, backs off from the daily fray and becomes the company thinker, analyzer, innovator, and catalyst for change.

Big businesses can afford to hire CEOs and consultants to think, strategize, and plan. For the rest of us, our survival and success depend on our ability—and determination—to think for ourselves.

> Articles about CEOs supposedly overpaid by chummy boards sell newspapers and magazines. Undeniably many pay packages do exceed all conception of human need.
>
> But smart boards recognize how much difference good direction at the top can make, and that hiring those abilities, even at brow-raising prices, is a relative bargain.

411

Thinking isn't doing nothing; it's doing the most important thing.

Business people are, by definition, busy. There are always more projects and ideas than time to execute them.

Most of us have trouble sitting still for deep and detailed thought. "Ready, fire, aim" better suits our personalities, and it works well for decisions with quick feedback and relatively small consequences.

But gut feel is rarely a smart shortcut in choosing strategic directions—it often leads to long and expensive detours and digressions. We can waste months or years of effort and expense learning what we might have thought out in hours or days.

Thinking takes time, but *not* thinking takes much more.

> "Few people think more than two or three times a year. I have made an international reputation for myself by thinking once or twice a week."
>
> **—George Bernard Shaw**

412

Break-even requires hard work; profitability requires smart work.

A lot of retailers work hard; their businesses usually survive and they're compensated moderately for their efforts. Competition assures that their compensation stays moderate—when it gets much above standard wages, competitors move in; when it falls below, competitors drop out. What these retailers have built is more a job than a business.

To build a business that returns more than hourly wages, we have to break out of the pack and create something unusual. We have to convert our understanding of the market into a new and profitable concept—something customers value and competitors can't easily replicate.

Easy to say, hard to do? Not really. The opportunities are infinitely more plentiful than the narrow range of existing retail models. They just aren't obvious while our noses are to the grindstone.

413

Doing a lot of things makes you busy; doing the right things makes you profitable.

We have an irresistible tendency to presume our profits are proportionate to our sales and activity. Consequently we feel the more sales and activity we're involved in the more profitable we'll be.

In truth some things we do make large profits while the many others make only losses. (If there is a business somewhere that makes a net profit on every product and activity, it's surely the result of exceptional analysis and discriminating selection and not happy accident.)

Increasing profits is often easy. We just need to analyze our products, activities, segments, and customers and choose carefully.

414

Good strategy starts with clear understanding of what produces the profit.

A profit analysis by product and activity shows exactly where money is being made. It's almost always our most reliable indicator of opportunity. Smart strategy is then simple: Do more of what's profitable and less of what's not.

The results of profit analysis are often so unexpected as to provoke disbelief. The losses generated by some products and activities defy all our business intuition; meanwhile previously underappreciated products and activities carry the company.

Sometimes the analysis suggests strategies contrary to what we might have preferred. The most profitable opportunities are rarely the easiest or the most personally attractive. Those are easy and attractive to everyone, and competition keeps profits low.

The true opportunities are those that offer us high, dependable, and defensible returns on our effort and investment. To recognize them, we have to do the numbers.

> "See first that the design is wise and just; that ascertained, pursue it resolutely."
>
> **—Shakespeare**

Bigger isn't better, better is better.

More sales mean more space, more employees, more inventory, more expenses, and more headaches—but not necessarily more profit.

Profit isn't a fixed percentage of each sale—its range is wide and includes more red numbers than black. The trick is to add sales that contribute profits and avoid sales that add only losses.

Growth is neither good nor bad. Profitable growth is good; unprofitable growth is bad.

You can't hunt two rabbits with one dog.

Youthful enthusiasm sometimes tempts us into markets and products on the fringes of our specialties. Opportunities for adding profitable business often look simple and ripe for the taking.

Occasionally the opportunities *are* worthwhile, but seldom are they as simple as they appear. And all are unavoidably distractions from our ongoing business.

We should remember that it's not whether we can do it, but whether we can do it best. Unless we're the customer's first choice, we don't get the sale. Small differences between first and second place competitors make huge differences in their profits.

Are we really so much smarter than our competitors that we can, with partial focus, beat them at what they focus on full-time?

In theory at least, it's not impossible for a company to compete and win in multiple markets or segments at once.

GE is essentially a holding company for many businesses, most of which, according to GE's selection criteria, dominate their markets. GE stock is among the bluest of "blue-chip" and had an unprecedented run of dependable and growing dividends.

Their key: operating each business separately, recruiting the highest quality proven managers for each, allowing the managers autonomy to operate their businesses, and judging results regularly and relentlessly through sound accounting.

They can hunt multiple rabbits because they have multiple dogs.

417

There's no right way to do a wrong thing.

Sometimes we're just spinning our wheels on projects, segments, customers, and businesses that have no future, regardless of how well we do them.

If a product or activity loses money, is not likely to become profitable with reasonable effort, and is not adding profits to related business, continuing it is only wasting time and resources.

Sure, it's tough jettisoning something we've worked hard on and invested heavily in. Pride isn't a tasty dish. Abandoning a business can feel like we're renouncing part of our identity.

But the decision is much easier when we remind ourselves that the more of it we do the more we lose.

Almost every market has a glut of guitar shops. Every wannabe rock star past his prime dreams of setting up shop where all day every day he can be the guru on the thing he knows and loves best. Golf, bike, camera, and sports shops have similar attraction for avid golfers, outdoor enthusiasts, shutterbugs, and high school jocks.

Because many try, average profits are typically negative. The shakeout is continuous, but there's a host of replacements standing on the sidelines ready to try their hands.

That's not to say that these businesses are impossible. But unless we can find some way to differentiate our stores from the perennial pack, we should expect continuous challenges and low returns.

Doing more of the thing you do best is a better bet than doing more things.

Doing many different things is sometimes lauded as "diversification." Its appeal is that when one product or industry fades or cycles downward, another is often on the upswing; thus a company with multiple products or in multiple industries hedges its bets.

Diversification is a proven strategy in investing—not for achieving high returns, but for improving the likelihood of stable returns. But diversification within a company divides management's time and leaves the company vulnerable to more focused competition.

Retailers who split their time managing businesses that are fundamentally different are fortunate to be profitable in any of them. Focusing on one profitable business and managing it well is almost always a more lucrative formula than trying to manage many.

> "The shoemaker makes a good shoe because he makes nothing else."
>
> **—Ralph Waldo Emerson**

> "The largest opportunity for any average man is right in the line where he is already established. When he is already in a business, no matter how far down the scale, he can go ahead faster in that business than he can in any other. The average man who, like myself, has no special gifts, does better to stick to the line he knows."
>
> **—Charles Walgreen**

Healthy growth requires periodic pruning.

Pruning is trimming the less useful to redirect energy and growth to the more desirable.

In retail, our time, effort, and capital are limited. When we choose to do one thing, it's necessarily at the expense of another.

A smart retailer regularly reviews not just whether the things he's doing are profitable, but whether they're the best opportunities available for his limited resources.

Forget about a level playing field and find your own field.

Any gathering of retailers includes lots of commiseration. Topics usually include manufacturers who give better prices to larger competitors, stores and Internet companies that don't have to collect sales taxes, retailers who sell for less by avoiding the expenses of showrooms and support, etc. If such injustices could be remedied, we reason, the contest would be fair and we could compete with anyone.

But equal isn't really what we need. When all else is equal, price is the only criterion and no one makes a profit.

What we need are differences—differences in products, knowledge, relationships, specialized services, convenience, terms, marketing, image, and any other criteria we can devise or create.

Among the most profound and useful business thought in recent years is Michael Porter's Five Forces of Competition. In his landmark book *Competitive Strategy,* he says that profits in a business are determined by:

- the intensity of rivalry
- the threat of substitutes
- the power of buyers
- the power of suppliers
- barriers to entry

Intensity of rivalry occurs in retailing, for example, when a market has multiple similar stores and their products are the same. As we well know, competitors in these situations lower prices until profits all but disappear.

The threat of substitutes refers to the potential of outside products to take the place of our product. For example, sales at CD stores dropped precipitously when music became downloadable.

The power of buyers refers to customers' ability to negotiate more advantageous pricing. Retail buyers have it when they collect extensive information on products, have multiple source options, or buy in bulk.

The power of suppliers refers to manufacturers' strength in the market. If a manufacturer's product is unique or his brand enjoys a strong reputation, the retailer is pressured to stock the product even if its pricing, margins, and terms are not favorable to the retailer.

Barriers to entry keep new competitors out. They occur in retail when, for example, the costs of opening a new store are high, saleable product isn't readily available, or the business is dependent on long-term relationships.

Considered together these five factors are impressively effective, not only in explaining the profitability of existing stores, but in predicting the profitability of new stores and opportunities.

The niche is your friend when you're small, your enemy when you've grown.

Big competitors are far less formidable when we take them on a piece at a time. It may not be possible to offer as much as they do, but it's usually not hard to offer some things better.

Specializing in a category can allow an impressive inventory of the chosen products. Specialized knowledge and attention to detail are rare enough in retail to attract a profitable piece of almost any market.

Niches are the Davids that Goliath retailers fear. They know that as they expand their markets and broaden their focus, opportunities increase for niche players to pick off segments. What were previously their competitive advantages—many stores, lots of employees, taught and entrenched methods of operation, established images, etc.—become legacies and liabilities that impede competitive responses.

We can wield the niches when we're small but have to guard against them as we grow.

At a time when Guitar Center was selling almost half the musical instruments in the U.S., independent retailers were feeling forlorn, forgotten, and highly vulnerable. An announcement that a Guitar Center store was coming to your market was like a sentence of death by slow torture.

Yet at this same time Guitar Center's CEO told me his greatest fear was small specialized retailers chipping away at his stores in individual markets until, one by one, his stores became unprofitable. He cited that as the demise of most large chains and feared his company might eventually succumb as well.

Abandon your mistakes as if they were someone else's.

Most business turnarounds are pretty simple—new management is brought in, makes an assessment of what's losing money, and eliminates it.

Why couldn't previous management do that? In most cases it's because they're too attached to the problems. Perhaps a loser was their pet project and it's embarrassing to quash something they've been a vocal proponent of. Perhaps they've become too entrenched in their rationalizations to recognize the truth. Or perhaps they have too much effort invested and can't bear the thought that it was wasted. So they hang on to their losers, even in the face of tremendous costs and risks to the company.

Mistakes are sunk costs. We have to forget the history, the investment, the time, and the pride as if they all were someone else's. We start with the situation as it is today and choose the best option from those in front of us.

If you had all the information, it wouldn't be a decision.

Waiting for enough information to make a decision indisputable is waiting too long—the opportunity is usually gone. We know the future only when it becomes the past.

Information is the basis for all decisions, but we have to judge how much and which information is practical. Then we weigh it, calculate the risks and rewards, and make our best educated guesses.

Indecision is a decision too, and seldom the one we prefer.

> A Taiwanese friend once told me, "To cross the river you've got to touch the stones." In other words, sometimes we've just got to get in and feel our way.

All business is gambling,
but double-or-nothing is soon nothing.

Entrepreneurs who risk everything and win big become business legends. Articles and books describe them as heroes and geniuses.

Not much is written about entrepreneurs who gamble big and lose. They're plentiful—more common than the winners—but their stories don't interest us. When their stories *are* written, it's usually how an errant and obsessive risk-taker followed a flawed and dangerous plan, created chaos, lost fortunes, ruined lives, and landed in jail. (Losses attract investigation and a good investigator can always find a law broken. Meanwhile the system is amazingly forgiving when everyone is happy with their profits.)

Everything we do in retail involves risk—opening the door for business each day is a gamble that the day's receipts will exceed its expenses. We can't build a store, hire an employee, place an order, or run an ad without taking a risk.

But these are calculated risks with affordable outcomes—rarely do they have catastrophic potential. When we spread our risks among multiple gambles with favorable odds and minimized potential for catastrophe, the law of probabilities keeps us out of trouble.

Gambling everything on every roll of the dice, regardless of the odds, guarantees disaster sooner or later.

Listen to the accountant always,
but exclusively never.

Numbers are our roadmap; they show us where we've been, where we are, and where we're going. Without them we'd be groping in the dark, lucky indeed to achieve the results we want.

But numbers don't tell the whole story. An accountant can tell us where expenses are disproportionate to sales, but seldom why. He can project the costs of a new product or venture, but not its market acceptance. He can total and forecast payroll expenses, but doesn't know if the correct people are employed. He can project the savings of eliminating an employee benefit, but not its effect on morale and retention.

These things aren't in the numbers; they require a feel for the market, products, operations, and people that comes only with hands-on retail experience.

Many big companies suffer notorious reputations (often deservedly) for impersonal policies and decisions, stiff and illogical rules, and uncaring attitudes. They are companies we love to hate.

The problem in almost all cases is that the decision makers are inundated with numbers and accounting, don't have enough contact and direct experience with customers, and don't trust their front-line employees.

A little less time with the accountants and a little more with customers would make them more human and less frustrating to deal with.

The best test of a plan is paper.

Some years ago the Harvard Business Review published a classic article entitled "Clear Writing Means Clear Thinking Means Clear Writing ..."

Putting thoughts and plans on paper does indeed refine (and sometimes contradict) them. It forces us to question the premises, fill in the gaps, predict the potentials, consider the possibilities, and assess the risks.

Sharing the document makes us more disciplined and thorough in its creation, assists in the detection of errors, and gets key personnel thinking along the same lines.

And discovering our errors on paper is considerably more efficient than living them.

Some expensive trial-and-error eventually convinced me of the prudence of thinking out on paper my (too prolific) schemes before imposing them on our company. Gradually we developed a format for sharing new ideas, and only after we had general consensus would we proceed.

Through the years we've saved these plans so when we occasionally wonder what we could have been thinking we can offer some evidence of sanity.

Reviewing them after the results are in has provided some great lessons—in retailing *and* humility.

If at first you do succeed,
try not to believe you're infallible.

Success is not a good teacher. Failure provides more useful lessons.

When success comes easily, we tend to underestimate future challenges and risks. We mistake good fortune for intelligence and invincibility; we forget that our time is limited and luck occasionally turns against us.

Periodic failures keep us realistic and help us appreciate our victories.

> "If people with unsolicited advice would just write a book we don't have to read, we'd gladly lie and say we did."
>
> —Chip Averwater
> (Thanks for reading)

I'd love to hear your thoughts!

chipaverwater@gmail.com

*I'd also be honored and grateful if you'd post
a review at amazon.com, bn.com,
or your favorite bookseller's website.*

Had some experience with a truth?
Tell us about it!

Disagree with a truth?
Let's discuss it!

Have some truths of your own?
We'd like to hear them!

We have a lot to talk about!

Join us at
www.retailtruths.com

Made in the USA
Middletown, DE
14 March 2015